Organizational Paradigm Shifts

National Association of College
and University Business Officers

Organizational Paradigm Shifts

National Association of College and University Business Officers

Library of Congress Cataloging-in-Publication Data

Organizational paradigm shifts.
   p. cm.
   Includes bibligraphical references
   ISBN 1-56972-001-0
   1. Education, Higher—United States—Administration.
2. Universities and colleges—United States—Business management.
I. National Association of College and University Business Officers.
LB2341.0827   1996   95-54020
378.1'00973—dc20   CIP

© 1996 National Association of College
and University Business Officers
One Dupont Circle, Suite 500
Washington, D.C. 20036

Printed in the United States of America.
Edited by Anne Kendrick
Cover design by Stacey Trey
   Cover photo courtesy of The Stock Market

Contents

Acknowledgments

Organizational Paradigm Shifts is made possible in part through a grant from Follett College Stores Fund for Financial Management. The fund, which was developed to help NACUBO satisfy the growing demand for cutting-edge financial management information, underwrites the development of various projects that address higher education financial management issues. NACUBO extends its appreciation to Scott Deaton, National Vice President of Marketing for Follett College Stores, who was instrumental in developing the fund and oversees its operation.

NACUBO also wishes to thank the contributors of *Organizational Paradigm Shifts*, whose names appear on their respective chapters and in the "About the Contributors" section on page 115. Other individuals who contributed to development of this book include Carol Campbell of Carleton College, Alice Handy of the University of Virginia, and William Merck of The College of William and Mary—all of whom reviewed the manuscript in its early stages; Sally V. Massy, of the Stanford Forum for Higher Education Futures, who edited chapter 7 and designed the charts in chapters 3 and 7; and Greer Glazer and Lawrence R. Kelley of Kent State University, who assisted the author in the development of chapter 4.

The team of NACUBO staff members who ushered this book from the conceptual stages to the printed page consisted of Stephanie Woodfork, who served as project manager; Robin Jenkins and Robert Shepko, who solicited authors and monitored the book's content; Anne Kendrick, who edited the manuscript; Stacey Trey, who oversaw design and production; and Dale Adams, who provided editorial assistance.

Preface

The word "paradigm," from the Greek word *paradigma*, means a pattern or map for understanding. Today we think of a paradigm as a set of rules, standards, laws, theories, and applications. In *The Structure of the Scientific Revolution*, Thomas Kuhn defined paradigms as "universally recognized scientific achievements that, for a time, provide model problems and solutions to a community of practitioners." (2nd ed., Chicago University Press, 1970.) Kuhn suggested that as science progresses, new discoveries occur that cause the paradigm to shift—in essence, changing the rules of the game.

For higher education, the discoveries that are changing the rules of the game are the quality tools such as process re-engineering and total quality management that many campuses are implementing. But the stronger forces of change are the growing demands institutions face to reduce costs, improve quality, and work harder to meet the needs of their customers.

Organizational Paradigm Shifts is a collection of essays that explore different methods of seeking, implementing, and coping with a new higher education paradigm. The authors—whose ranks include presidents, provosts, and chief financial officers from large and small institutions, as well as higher education consultants—share their varied experiences of implementing change on campus.

In chapter 1, I draw from my own experiences at two research universities—Oregon State University and University of California at Santa Cruz—and from my earlier published works on total quality management and business process re-engineering to describe the emerging management paradigm on today's campuses. This chapter explores the need for a new paradigm in higher education, covers the steps that institutions need to take to achieve change, and provides guidance on managing change once it occurs.

Mary Jo Maydew of Mount Holyoke College offers a perspective on consortial relationships in chapter 2. Maydew uses her own experience as a member of the Five Colleges, Inc., consortium to explore how other institutions, especially small colleges and universities, can reduce costs, improve productivity, and increase buying power through consortia.

In chapter 3, Jillinda Kidwell of Coopers & Lybrand and David O'Brien of Stanford University illustrate how higher education's common problem of administrative inefficiency can be solved through process re-engineering. The chapter also offers a description of how Stanford's School of Medicine is using re-engineering tools to re-think its administrative structure.

Myron Henry of Kent State University shares his institution's re-structuring and reallocation experiences in chapter 4. Henry describes the needs, processes, and outcomes of change at Kent State and offers his list of the top 10 issues that his institution and others must address.

In chapter 5, Gerard Shaw of Coopers & Lybrand and Paula Rooney, president of Dean College, team up to describe student affairs' changing paradigm. Shaw and Rooney chart the ways in which the role of student affairs has transformed over the years in response to changes in economic climate and the demands of customers.

In chapter 6, Patrick Keating et al. describe Carnegie Mellon University's struggle to succeed in a competitive marketplace and the service improvements and new vision that resulted from this struggle. The authors explain Carnegie Mellon's attempts to reduce its administrative component by focusing on work processes such as financial management, information services, and sponsored research support services.

In chapter 7, University of Michigan President James Duderstadt describes the dilemma of the modern research university: the danger of becoming a complex corporate conglomerate that dilutes its core business. Admitting that higher education has demonstrated a remarkable inability to eliminate obsolete activities, Duderstadt challenges the reader to imagine a new university whose motto is "to create, preserve, integrate, transmit, and apply knowledge."

As the chapters of this book illustrate, it is very unlikely that colleges and universities will develop a singular model for achieving a competitive edge in today's market. However, a common set of priorities does exist around which all institutions must redesign or re-engineer. These priorities are the focus of *Organizational Paradigm Shifts*. They include moving toward a process-oriented structure, using teams as work units, sharing responsibilities and accountability between central administration and colleges, using new technology, reducing the size of administration, creating a fault-tolerant environment where risk-taking is encouraged, and taking advantage of volume discounts.

L. Edwin Coate, Ph.D.
Vice President of Business Services
MiraCosta Community College

Beyond Re-engineering: Changing the Organizational Paradigm

1

L. Edwin Coate

Historically, changes occur through the following sequence of events: presence of sufficient dissatisfaction with things as they are, creation of a clear vision of a final goal, development of a strategy for change to achieve the desired state, and attainment of the knowledge and skills to achieve the change. This chapter explores the need for change in higher education, describes an emerging management paradigm that will enable colleges and universities to achieve change, and provides instruction for managing change once it has been implemented.

Taking the Steps Toward Change

The landscape of higher education in the United States has changed dramatically over the last 40 years. The number of institutions has grown from 1,800 to 3,300, and enrollment has exploded from 2.7 million to nearly 14 million students, with no end in sight.

This tremendous growth has been fueled by a number of factors, including demographics, economic prosperity, and society's goal of creating greater access to educational opportunities. The demographic boom slowed in the early to mid-1970s, but federal grants kept enrollment high by expanding access to a broader segment of students. Resourceful management in colleges and universities and general prosperity staved off the anticipated problems of the 1980s, but the expected wave of difficulties eventually took effect in the early 1990s. Spiraling costs and tuition, cutbacks in financial aid, and the undertow of a national recession eroded state budgets, institutional operating budgets, capital, and quality.

The current situation is one of dissatisfaction that includes poor public perception, budget deficits, higher tuition, reduced demand, and growing gloom in the industry. The general perception is that tuition has hit a level of resistance—if not a ceiling—that will limit higher education's ability to pass further cost increases along to students and parents. At the same time, financial aid has shifted from grants to loans, raising questions about how students will pay for higher education in the future. Students are signaling that they have reached their limit in terms of their (or their parent's) ability to pay. Many individuals from all walks of life are re-examining the value of the product in the light of its high cost.

Recognizing a Need

Cost pressures have led to increased scrutiny of institutional management as well as re-examination of the value of higher education. Observers outside the realm of higher education believe opportunity exists for significant improvement in the way colleges and universities manage their programs and operations. The future presents a variety of options to higher education, some that are painful but promising and some that are downright depressing.

Many people have pointed to healthcare as an industry that has faced similar problems of over-capacity, increased public concern over rising costs, and increased government regulation and oversight. Like access to healthcare, access to higher education has long been an important part of the American dream. Both industries serve and employ millions of individuals and directly influence the cost and capability of the labor force on which all other American industries depend. Unfortunately, the experience of the healthcare industry does not help to dispel the gloom in administrative circles on campus. Instead, it forebodes yet more intrusion and regulatory oversight as demanding consumers, employers, and taxpayers call for accountability in the face of institutional failure to contain costs.

In spite of its difficulties, however, American higher education is the envy of the world. But this advantage could weaken as our colleges and universities grapple with economic realities. Research, once the private bastion of academia, is increasingly being conducted in the private sector by companies that have already re-engineered their processes. The challenge to higher education is to sustain its advantage in the face of acute financial problems that could undermine all that has been created over the last centuries.

There is a strong need for institutional and industry leadership and, in many respects, a unique opportunity for positive change. The critical nature of the situation creates an opportunity to make difficult choices and weakens some of the old resistance to new approaches. True dissatisfaction exists with the way things are, and the higher education industry is ready for change.

Creating a New Vision

The development of a clear vision for a final goal is a critical success factor in fostering organizational change. Getting higher education faculty, administrators, and their staff to embrace radical change that will directly affect their work lives is not easy. Employees must be presented with a compelling argument for change, and then given a clear goal or vision statement on which to focus so that change can be achieved.

Once a clear and simple message is developed, it should be shared with every member of the staff and faculty, and repeated over and over. The first part of the message should convey where the institution currently is and why it cannot stay there; the second part should describe what the institution wants to become.

The first communication must convey a forceful message that change is essential to the future of the campus: If budget cuts are necessary, the institution will still be able to provide better service to faculty and students by simplifying processes. If the campus does not face budget cuts, savings can be used to enhance competitiveness by improving teaching, adding new and exciting classes to the curriculum, or reducing tuition and fees. The second message, articulating what the university needs to become, gives employees a vision for which to strive. Articulating the vision forces management to think clearly about the purpose and outcome of the change.

Leaders' responsibility is to communicate the need to change the campus organization. Existing staff and faculty will not want to hear that the old culture does not work anymore, because many of them played a substantial role in creating that campus organization. So diplomacy and credibility are needed to communicate a clear case for the vision and the action.

Developing a Strategy

Once a clear vision is articulated, a strategy for change must be developed. The concept of creating value and passing it along to customers is a new management strategy that can transform rigid institutions into responsive, world-class colleges and universities.

Without students to teach, research to conduct, or services to provide, colleges and universities have no business. Without value, customers have no reason to choose one institution over an increasingly large number of similar institutions. Competition, market niche, empty seats, and empty beds are a new phenomenon in higher education, yet these problems have long been familiar to American businesses.

Customers should feel that they have received exceptional value for their dollar. When tuition was heavily subsidized, almost any level of teaching was considered valuable. But with the cost of tuition skyrocketing, that value is now being scrutinized and questioned. To be customer driven, institutions must be able to read their customers' minds, give them caring, personalized service, and provide them with the knowledge and skills they need to be successful. No small task!

All businesses know that retaining good customers is much less costly than capturing new ones or recapturing ones previously lost. If higher education does not control its costs and rethink its programs, markets could be lost that would be prohibitively expensive to recapture. But just who are the customers? Students, faculty, taxpayers, parents, legislators, and citizens are some of them. The trick to being customer driven is to first recognize the customers, then identify their needs, and subsequently, meet or exceed their expectations.

Higher education's strategy for change must also include a shift away from emphasis on tasks, employees, and structures, and toward a new focus on processes. Today's universities and colleges, as well as private sector companies such as insurance firms and computer chip manufacturers, were all built around the ideas of the division or specialization of labor and the consequent fragmentation of work. The larger the organization, the more specialized and fragmented the work.

At most colleges and universities, registration, admissions, purchasing, and facilities management offices typically assign separate staff to process standardized forms. They enter data and pass the forms on to supervisors for approval. The supervisor subsequently sends the form to another office for more data to be entered or sometimes for all the data to be re-entered. No one completes the entire job; each just performs piecemeal tasks. As these processes mature and evolve, redundancy is built in along with control checks. Many processes now exceed 50 percent in non-value-added work in higher education organizations.

On today's campuses, staff may talk about serving customers, but the real job is still perceived as keeping the boss happy. Many employees feel they are just a cog in the wheel. When things go wrong, it is the manager's job to solve the problem. In turn, the manager is evaluated by the number of direct reports and the size of the budget he or she has. The one with the biggest empire wins.

W. Edwards Deming realized that the United States' way of organizing work was ineffective. In his research, he found that 85 percent of the problems in organizations were occurring in processes, not people.[1] But his key strategy of focusing on process improvement presented a problem for U.S. management because most work is managed by focusing on tasks, jobs, people, and structures—not processes. Deming introduced process management in Japan in the early 1950s, and Japan's business success since World War II is often attributed to this strategy.

Process management asks organizations to realize that customers pay the salaries—and that they must provide a product or service that meets or exceeds customer expectations. All employees must accept ownership of problems and actively participate in resolving them. Employees belong on teams—they fail or succeed together.

Quality Process Management

Most institutions of higher education have developed around a bureaucratic organizational model. This model is hierarchial, procedural, and dependent on specialization of labor, narrow delegation of authority, and complex procedures. The problems associated with this model include—

- substantial organization layering,
- a high reliance on paper and forms to document decisions and transactions,
- excessive points of control, and
- excessive redundancy of operations.

Within the bureaucratic model, a proliferation of unnecessary tasks significantly reduces productivity, while communication is blocked by vertical functional silos.

To foster productivity and service, a new model is evolving on many college and university campuses. Built on the concept of process control, this new model has evolved from implementing the new management tools of total quality management (TQM) and business process re-engineering (BPR). This emerging model is quality process management.

Quality process management is a disciplined, structural approach designed to meet or exceed the needs of the customer by improving the efficiency and effectiveness of processes. This new model reflects the strategies of many industrial leaders, but only a very few campuses. It is meant to eliminate layers of hierarchy by decentralizing the authority for decision making, increasing spans of control, and imbedding minimal internal controls within integrated information systems.

The quality process management model delegates responsibility and authority to the lowest possible organizational level, where the customer first interacts with the institution. It encompasses a set of human resource strategies that specifies expected employee behavior and rewards risk taking, initiative, personal accountability, outcomes, collaboration, and customer service. The model uses process improvement teams to improve processes and rewards teams accordingly.

A process is a sequence of activities intended to achieve a result (create added value) for a customer. A typical college or university has more than 150 processes in place. There are academic processes, which include teaching, research, technology transfer, and tenure giving; auxiliary processes, such as food service, child care, mail service, and book sales; and business and administrative processes, such as fund raising, hiring, assigning space, allocating money, cleaning and maintenance of buildings, and distribution of payments.

The Diagnostic

Quality process management begins by identifying processes that do *not* add much value for the customer. A diagnostic is conducted through simple brainstorming by a core team of the best and brightest staff and faculty, who look at the work outputs needed to meet the mission of the institution. Each critical process should be reviewed in terms of output volume, resource costs, customer satisfaction, and customer importance. A diagnostic matrix should then be developed as shown in figure 1-1.

Processes with high output volume, high costs, low customer satisfaction, and high customer importance are candidates for the radi-

Figure 1-1: Sample Process Evaluation Matrix

Process	Output Volume	Resource Costs	Customer Sastisfaction	Customer Importance	Willingness To Change
Aquire Goods	High	High	Low	High	High
Financial Transaction	Very High	High	Low	High	High
Manage Facilities	Medium	High	Low	High	Medium
Contracts & Grants Mgt.	Medium	Medium	Medium	High	Medium
Curriculum Development	Low	Low	Medium	High	Low

cal redesign of BPR. Processes with low output volume, low cost, and moderate satisfaction would benefit from the more gentle approach of TQM.

Process Mapping

After processes have been identified and diagnosed, those needing attention should then be "mapped." Process mapping establishes an "as is" baseline by tracing the path of a service or product request through the organization, culminating in an output delivered to an external customer. Overall, the objective of process mapping is to understand the process—the activities, inputs, outputs, resources, costs and value-added work versus non-value-added work. (See figure 1-2.)

The process map (or flow chart) is a visual aid, a way of recording each activity in a process. Mapping begins when team members physically report to the department where work originates and then "walk" each activity through its part of the process. Team members observe and record the first activity in the process, then observe and record the physical flow of the paperwork or product. They subsequently identify the use and value of the activity's output. This step is repeated for each activity in the process.

Once the process map is completed, the team members go back and add touch time (the amount of time an employee actually works on the transaction), lag time (the amount of time it takes for the

Figure 1-2: Sample Process Map

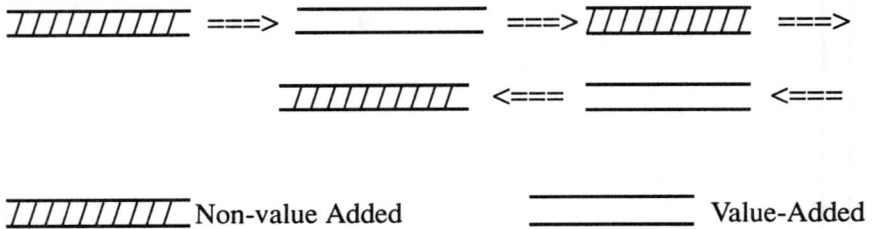

///////// Non-value Added   ——————— Value-Added

paperwork to go to the next step), and the error rate. Finally, the team determines whether each activity is value-added (an activity required by a customer that the customer is willing to pay for) or non-value-added (an activity that can be eliminated by technology or is simply unnecessary).

Each process activity is analyzed by asking the following questions:

- What is being done?
- Is it necessary?
- Can it be eliminated?
- What are the major bottlenecks?
- Where is the work done and/or who does it?
- Is the work done manually?
- How long does it take?
- What are the costs?
- What is the workload?
- What is the quality?
- When and how does the customer interface with the process?

The key issues and questions are then summarized and listed under six headings on a cause-and-effect or "fishbone" diagram, as shown in figure 1-3.

By adding up touch time and lag time and identifying both non-value-added work and the number of people that actually touch each form across campus, a business case for improvement can be developed. For each process, total full-time equivalent (FTE) employees and costs are determined and both non-value-added work and estimated savings are identified. A sample business case is provided in figure 1-4.

This data allows team members to prioritize process redesign efforts and determine which process improvement tool—BPR, TQM, or both—is appropriate.

Figure 1-3: Fishbone Diagram

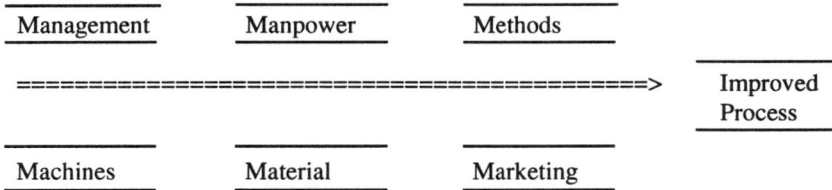

Management	Manpower	Methods	
==>			Improved Process
Machines	Material	Marketing	

Figure 1-4: Building the Business Case

Process	FTE	Total Estimated Costs	Non-value Added	Estimated Savings
Acquire Goods	90	$4.1M	52-71%	$1.8M
Record Transaction	120	$5.2M	30-100%	$1.7M
Manage Facilities	72	$7.4M	9-23%	$1.1M
Hire Employees	80	$3.4M	11-23%	$0.5M

Total Quality Management

TQM is a commitment to excellence by everyone in an organization—excellence achieved through teamwork and a process of continuous improvement. It requires dedication to being the best at delivering high quality services that meet or exceed customer expectations. TQM is a structural procedure for creating organizationwide participation in planning and implementing a continuous improvement process that meets or exceeds the expectations of the customer. It is built on the Deming assumption that 85 percent of problems are process problems.

Teams are the heart of the TQM process, which is based on the belief that better solutions emerge when everyone is given a chance to work on process problems. Just as important, solutions are accepted and implemented more quickly and are longer lasting because the people affected have helped develop them. TQM teams should consist of people who normally work together on the process being reviewed. The team examines a process that can be improved by utilizing resources they already control. Each team includes a team leader (most often the supervisor of the process being reviewed), a facilitator or trainer, and no more than 10 team members. The team sponsor (usually the team leader's boss), ensures that the team's work is guided by the institution's vision.

TQM teams use a 10-step problem-solving model to complete their work:

- **Step One:** Identify and interview customers of the process to determine which services are not meeting their needs.
- **Step Two:** Chart customer problems, select one major problem to work on, prepare an issue statement to direct the study, and use customer data to set a measure of improved performance.
- **Step Three:** Construct detailed flow charts and process maps of the process and subprocesses as they currently exist.
- **Step Four:** Brainstorm possible causes of the process problem, then use TQM tools to select critical causes for further study.
- **Step Five:** Collect data, graph it concisely, and use it to determine root causes of the customer problem. This data becomes a benchmark for measuring future progress.
- **Step Six:** Develop possible solutions for the root causes that are verified by data, then measure them against criteria that reflect customer needs.
- **Step Seven:** Identify benchmarks for the process being studied (e.g., processes used by other organizations or work areas that produce a high quality product or service). Measure possible solutions against the benchmarks created.
- **Step Eight:** Implement the best solutions, monitor their performance, and adopt those that work.
- **Step Nine:** Measure the results of the improvement and refine performance measures. If the problems are solved, turn the "fixes" into standard operating procedures.
- **Step Ten:** Select another process to review and improve.

TQM is a slow, deliberate way to improve work processes. It is transitional and fits in well with the academic culture. Process improvements are often small and build up incrementally over time. Many organizations take over five years to achieve truly significant change.

Within the quality process management model, TQM is used for processes that are not broken but can be improved. Most processes contain at least 30 percent non-value-added work; TQM is very effective in improving these processes over time. Experience to date shows that over 70 percent of work processes in academic institutions can benefit from this form of process improvement. Results show an average cost and cycle time reduction of approximately 10 percent per process over a three-year period.

Business Process Re-engineering

BPR is the fundamental rethinking and radical redesign of processes. Its goal is to achieve dramatic improvements in critical measures of performance, such as cost, quality, service and speed.[2] Some say BPR means simply "starting over." As it relates to higher education, BPR means asking the question, "If we were recreating the university or college, given what we now know and given current technology, what would it look like?" Re-engineering a university means throwing out old systems and processes, going back to the beginning and inventing a better way of doing things. In quality terms, re-engineering is used to achieve major breakthroughs in areas identified by strategic planning.

How does a university re-engineer its processes, both business and academic? Where do the ideas for radical change come from? Although many corporations are using BPR, to date only four or five universities have real experience in this area. Information technology (IT) is often the enabler for re-engineering processes. But BPR does not mean simply automating existing work, or repaving the cow paths. Instead, IT allows for data to be entered only once and sent quickly where it needs to go so that meaningful analysis and strategic planning can take the place of repetitive work.

BPR is the most creative part of the quality process management model. Re-engineering asks the process team to abandon the familiar and search for the unknown. It demands imagination and vision. Team members are asked to forget about rules, regulations, policies, and commonly held institutional values.

Re-engineering teams use a nine-step problem-solving model to guide their redesign work:

- **Step One:** Identify and interview customers of the process selected to be re-engineered to find out which services are really needed and which are not meeting customer expectations.
- **Step Two:** Construct a detailed flow chart of the process and all subprocesses as they currently exist.
- **Step Three:** Brainstorm new innovative ways to provide needed services to the customer. Develop a new process map that identifies a radical redesign of the process.
- **Step Four:** Identify "best in class" processes used by other universities and business organizations. Measure performance by "best in class" organizations and benchmark against the new redesign.
- **Step Five:** Develop needed system architecture to support the redesigned process. Prepare a request for proposals (RFP) and select a vendor.
- **Step Six:** Develop an action plan for implementation.
- **Step Seven:** Develop a training plan for new skills needed by staff and any displaced or reassigned staff members.
- **Step Eight:** Oversee implementation of redesigned process.
- **Step Nine:** Measure results and modify process as necessary.

Quality Process Leadership

Quality process management is an exciting new way to improve the quality of work performed for customers. It places the customer at the top of the organization and compels leaders to provide direction, empowerment, and support for the people who create value for customers.

Quality process management requires significant changes in the prevailing organizational culture that all begin with leadership. Leadership is required to reduce fear of change, encourage open communications, push decision making to the lowest practical level and build performance around systems that motivate people to grow and develop.

Leadership in a quality university or college is essential to create the vision and provide the direction that will unify and inspire these efforts. A compelling vision has the power to motivate. Clear communication of campus direction focuses energies and talents on the shared purpose and common goals of quality process management.

Leadership helps determine these shared goals and translate them into action. Quality process management provides the planning structure and implementation that can help leaders focus and direct their energies to improve critical processes. Leadership ensures that appropriate organizational change occurs, allowing form to follow function.

Managing the Organizational Change

> *I have not failed 10,000 times,*
> *I have successfully found 10,000 ways that do not work.*
> —Thomas A. Edison

Colleges and universities do change, but change often occurs haphazardly and not by virtue of any managerial decision or plan. Much of the literature on organizational change emphasizes the issues of planning (i.e., human resistance to change and using leverage from the top to get those at a lower level to behave differently), yet experience shows that random acts exclusive of strategic planning are the norm.

For every combination of vision, leadership style, and process restructuring, there is an organizational structure that will work, and many that will not. The question is how to decide what new structure is needed and when to implement it. Finding a workable arrangement of roles and work processes can be a real struggle.

Adjusting to a major managerial paradigm change such as quality process management will inevitably require some organizational realignment as the organization responds to a new vision, new technology, and new work processes. The implementation of new information technology alone requires reorganizational response. New technologies create pressure to decentralize, which has both structural and political implications.

In *Complex Organizations: A Critical Essay*, C. Perrow says that "organizational structure needs to be responsive to organizational purpose, and the shape of an organization should be determined by its goals, technologies and environment."[3] So if goals are changing to be more efficient and effective, technologies are changing from batch processing to on-line processing, and work processes and the external environment are moving toward less government support and more accountability, then it stands to reason that the organization or culture will change as well. Major organizational change efforts typically generate the following issues:

- Change has a significant effect on individual employees who need to feel valued, effective, and in control, but may instead feel incompetent, needy, and powerless.
- Change requires new kinds of structured alignments that will not leave employees confused and uncertain.
- Change may cause conflict among those who think they will benefit and those who are afraid they will not.
- Change can create a sense of loss.

Organizational change efforts may fail at first if top management overemphasizes rationality and underestimates the power of resistance by lower level employees. Employees often have good reasons for resisting change—no one enjoys feeling incompetent or powerless. Changes in practice, procedures, or routine patterns may undercut employees' ability to perform. Further, if staff is simply told to make changes without being told why, they may feel puzzled or powerless.

Individual skills and confidence are not the only important issue of organizational change. Structural problems can also block change efforts. The formal structure of any new organizational change must provide a clarity of roles, predictability, and some degree of security. New roles must prescribe duties and how work is to be performed in the redesigned process. New policies and procedures must synchronize various efforts and coordinate actions.

One way to implement a new organizational paradigm on campus is to form a BPR team that focuses on four strategies: restructuring, retraining, development of service centers, and recruiting. Each of these strategies is described below.

Restructuring

The first step in restructuring is to review and evaluate roles, reporting relationships, organizational span of control, management accountability, and the number of management layers. Such issues may include an assessment of the work process and decision-making processes within the current organizational structure. The team should consider the possibility of allowing more decisions to be made at lower levels in the organization, supported by strong control rather than surrounded by redundant oversight.

Opportunities for organizational change at a college or university may include the following:

- Creating "service centers" to delegate down authority and provide business services, developing economies of scale in service delivery.
- Reducing levels of management to increase the span of control and improve efficiency.
- Ensuring that form follows function when work processes are changed.

Service Centers. Service centers cluster an appropriate volume of work by consolidating the administrative functions of smaller units to promote regular use of on-line systems and frequent applications of related policies and procedures. These centers facilitate communications and put similar work together, allowing a shared responsibility among similarly trained and skilled individuals. They also establish an organizational structure that provides appropriate separation of duties and effectively handles delegated authority, decentralized processes, and new legislation as it occurs. Finally, service centers establish formal levels of accountability.

Duties of service centers can range from advising managers based on knowledge of policies and procedures, to preparing related paperwork, entering information on-line, and maintaining accurate records. Customers of service centers expect skill levels which include analysis, execution of budget plans as provided by unit managers, and the expertise to process on-line transactions such as payroll, personnel, and financial information. The key to the successful operation of service centers is a clear delineation between the responsibilities of the service center and those of the unit manager.

The service center manager is a business manager who is responsible for overseeing the smooth functioning of a service center that supports several units, such as accounting, material management, fire, police, and hazardous materials. Much like managing an accounting firm that handles the accounts of many small businesses, a service center manager is responsible for the accurate and timely execution of decisions made by these units. The service center manager is accountable for ensuring that policies and procedures are appropriately followed, that staff in the service center understand these policies and procedures, and that transactions are processed correctly. But unit managers retain the ultimate authority for their businesses, making sound business decisions based on information provided by the service center.

Retraining

Investments in restructuring must be matched with collateral investments in training. Process redesign has powerful implications for crucial skills. For example, planners must become more collaborative, computer analysts need new computer language skills, and accountants need new computer skills.

Typically, the framework for employee training at colleges and universities offers random opportunities to interested employees at random times, rather than providing a coherent curriculum designed to teach skills required by new automated work processes, reinforce service values, and assist employees in assuming increased responsibilities. Solutions to this problem may include the following:

- Assign responsibility for development of core competencies curriculum and make campus employees responsible for technical training in their areas.
- Create training and development certificate programs based on core competencies for service center employees.
- Reduce the number of job classifications by 80 percent.
- Develop reward systems based on accomplishments.

Recruiting

Another way of dealing with change is to bring in new blood. Although existing staff are often loyal and willing to learn new skills, bringing in new employees that already have experience in leading change and new computer language allows an organization to "jump start" the effort.

In almost all re-engineering efforts, recruiting new employees can be an effective tool in dealing with change. In a world of rapid change and uncertainty, organizations need some order, predictability, and perceived meaning. With a skillful mix of restructuring, retraining, and recruiting, campuses should be able to function in a competitive world that offers greater opportunity and enhanced risk.

Conclusion

Implementing proactive change management in the administrative culture of a higher education institution is no easy task. It is tremendously difficult to persuade the people within the university to embrace the prospect of such a cultural change and accept the idea that their jobs will undergo radical transformation. The effort becomes an educational and communications campaign from beginning to end.

Continuing research on organizational culture, coupled with the development of instruments to measure it, has provided convincing evidence that the concept offers significant insights into the functioning of organizations. Organizational culture can be generally viewed as "the ways of thinking, behaving, and believing that members of a social unit have in common."[4] Culture is the shared values and beliefs that guide the way members of the campus community behave toward each other and approach their work. Moving from a passive, defensive style to a constructive style focusing on self-actualization, achievement, and humanistic encouragement is a difficult, time-consuming task.

Once an organization begins to shift toward a new paradigm, the following things will begin to happen:

- Workers' roles change from controlled to empowered.
- Work is performed where it makes sense, work steps are performed in a logical order, and redundant tasks are eliminated.
- Checks and controls are significantly reduced.
- Jobs change from simple to complex.
- Work units change from functional departments to process teams.
- Values change from protective to productive.
- Organizational structures change from hierarchical to flat.
- Salary structures change from salaries based on the size of budget and staff to salaries based on results.
- Systems change from paving cow paths to enabling radical changes.
- Work is performed for the customer, not the business.

This is a significant paradigm shift from the bureaucratic model currently in use at most colleges and universities today.

One of the enduring characteristics of our national university system has been its stability. But that stability has a tremendous downside: It becomes an excuse to resist change. To believe that we can preserve the American university as it is today is to ignore the reality of our rapidly changing world and its expectations of us. However, change of the magnitude required today can only be made with the use of new methodologies combined with strong leadership and administrative support. Quality process management is an exciting new management tool that leads to a new organizational paradigm offering significant improvement over the current bureaucratic model used by most institutions of higher education.

Notes

1. W. Edwards Demings, *Out of the Crisis* (Cambridge, Mass.: Massachusetts Institute of Technology Press, 1986).
2. M. Hammer and J. Champy, *Re-engineering the Corporation* (New York: Harper Collins, 1993).
3. C. Perrow, *Complex Organizations: A Critical Essay*, 3rd ed. (New York: Random House, 1986).
4. K. Roberts, C. Hulin, and D. Rousseau, *Developing an Interdisciplinary Science of Organizations* (San Francisco: Jossey-Bass Publishers, 1978).

Thinking About Consortia   2

Mary Jo Maydew

For large universities and small colleges alike, topics like downsizing, restructuring, and re-engineering permeate nearly every conference, publication, and conversation on the subject of higher education. But how much cost reduction can an institution achieve—whether by doing less or improving productivity—and still be able to offer high quality programs and services to an increasingly consumer-oriented student population? The challenge of staying competitive is a particularly difficult one for small institutions, which generally have fewer resources and experience less growth. Some small institutions have the financial strength and drawing power to continue as separate and insular institutions; others will merge, be absorbed by a stronger school, or ultimately cease to exist.

The purpose of this chapter is to explore another way of facing this challenge: collaboration. Consortial relationships can be advantageous to any institution, but they are particularly powerful options for small colleges. Cooperative efforts among institutions can take many forms, from the simplest and most peripheral program expansions to intricate, integrated programs and services. In the discussion that follows, Five Colleges, Inc.—the 26-year-old consortium to which Mount Holyoke College, the University of Massachusetts at Amherst, Amherst, Hampshire, and Smith Colleges belong—is used as an example to describe the various layers of cooperation involved in a consortial relationship.

Stages of Cooperation

The cooperative efforts among the institutions that would become members of Five Colleges, Inc., began before the 1970 founding of Hampshire College. As early as the mid-1960s, a number of informal agreements were in place among these neighboring institutions, primarily in areas of academic cooperation. Formal collaboration as Five Colleges continued this focus on program enrichment activities and culminated in a joint department of astronomy. Students were permitted to cross-register in classes at any of the five institutions, with a free Five College bus route to transport them among the campuses. New joint academic programs were developed in areas such as ethnic and regional studies, international relations, early music, and coastal and marine sciences. A Five College department of dance was added in 1976. Although this cooperation permitted cost-efficient expansion into new and innovative curricular areas, this first layer of collaboration increased rather than reduced overall costs for the individual institutions.

Along with these academic ventures, deeper levels of cooperation were developing that involved pooling expertise and combining purchasing power. Early in the history of Five Colleges, a faculty borrowing program was developed that streamlined leave replacements and the adding of extra course sections. This program also reduced duplication in the purchasing of expensive and infrequently used pieces of equipment, which can be shared among consortium members. Special expertise is also shared: At a reasonable cost, the University of Massachusetts provides nuclear safety services for all members and student health center services for the other Amherst-based institutions. Mount Holyoke and Smith share the services and costs of an environmental health and safety officer. This kind of joint effort produces a combination of cost reduction and cost avoidance. If the cooperative efforts are the first solution to a new or expanded need, the combined program avoids the higher costs of individual programs. If individual programs are developed first and a joint effort follows, an actual reduction in existing costs can be achieved.

Joint purchasing has saved all five participating institutions enormous amounts of money over the years. Some joint purchasing initiatives—in areas such as equipment, computers, and some kinds of supplies—are very long-standing. Others, such as insurance coverages, health insurance, workers' compensation, and student loan processing are new but very promising. Many additional opportunities exist in the area of joint purchasing, including such possibilities as legal and accounting services, food and paper goods, and other benefits coverages.

Another kind of joint purchasing involves sharing the costs of training and development. At Five Colleges, this type of sharing has occurred in such areas as health and safety programs, training for total quality management teams and facilitators, design and presentation of management training programs, and development of a training program for campus security officers. Again, many other possibilities exist, from interviewing skills workshops for students to understanding the vast potential of the World Wide Web.

The next level of cooperation penetrates more deeply into how the individual institutions function. One example is combining databases to provide consortium-wide information for the campus communities. At Five Colleges, the first such collaboration was a joint electronic library catalog, which was developed in the early 1980s. More recent efforts include combined on-line course catalogs and career services library collections, and other projects, such as a combined on-line inventory of the museum collections, are in the planning stages. These efforts tend not to reduce costs directly, since individual campuses are unlikely to have already had such systems in place. However, they do provide a cost-effective way of doing together what competitive pressures would eventually force institutions to do on their own at greater total cost.

A second example of this functional type of cooperation is sharing staff and programs at a level short of actually combining operations. Five Colleges is beginning to move in this direction in areas such as recycling and risk management and insurance. The Five College recycling program involves three years of shared funding for a joint position whose duties are to build awareness, develop individual institutional expertise in recycling, and identify joint and individual opportunities for reducing or controlling costs. Once this happens, the position is expected to be eliminated and the benefits to continue.

Risk management and insurance is a different kind of joint program, in which a shared Five College risk manager position has been created to oversee the insurance purchases of the four private colleges and provide expert assistance to the campuses in risk avoidance. This position has in its first year resulted in considerable net savings to the campuses. Other shared staff positions are in the planning stage, including a Five College coordinator of information technology to assist the consortium in thinking about and organizing the many opportunities for joint efforts in information technology.

Inevitably, the next layer of cooperation will be the actual sharing of operations. Five Colleges has already developed some expertise in combined operations, particularly on the academic side, through the joint programs and departments now in place. Future opportunities, both academic and administrative, seem limited only by the imagination. Combined payroll operations, computer centers, purchasing offices, and other "back office" functions are just a few of the many possibilities. Equally imaginable are continuing combinations among small academic departments, such as classics, religion, physics, and some languages. The five physics departments have already begun rotating advanced-level elective courses among the institutions rather than teaching the same course on each campus, which frees a faculty member to participate in other curricular efforts. It is important to recognize, however, that joining existing functions is enormously different—and considerably more difficult—than establishing a new shared function. All of the difficulties of re-engineering on an individual campus are multiplied several-fold when the challenge of coping with different campus cultures and more complex approval and authority structures is combined with the individual territoriality and group anxiety that such changes inevitably ignite.

Some Organizational Issues for Consortia

Consortia, like multi-campus systems, have organizational issues that are particularly characteristic of their structures. And while each consortium will develop its own unique set of solutions, these characteristic issues are likely to emerge wherever efforts at cooperation begin or intensify.

One issue that surfaced early in the Five Colleges experience was cost sharing. This might have become a highly contentious issue, particularly since the participating institutions are so different from one another. In addition, the opportunity for creating elaborate and complicated cost-sharing mechanisms was clearly present. It is a tribute to the Five Colleges collaborators of a generation ago that good sense and generosity prevailed and the resulting system of cost sharing is simple, stable, and equitable. In the Five Colleges system, no costs are transferred when students at one campus take courses at another. This policy has vastly simplified the collaboration, has not resulted in significant abuse, and has served the consortium well for 26 years. Joint programs are paid for through a straightforward system of equal cost sharing. This has ensured that there are no senior or junior partners and that every institution has an equal voice in the work of the consortium. Keeping it simple has worked very well for Five Colleges, Inc.

Another issue that arises quickly and re-emerges regularly relates to participation in any particular project. The rigidity embodied in the "all or nothing" mindset regarding collaborative efforts is likely to limit the possibilities for joint programs and, perhaps even more significantly, generally discourage the openmindedness and flexibility that are central to successful consortial activity. Insisting on involving all members of the group in each project will limit the collaboration's accomplishments, particularly when the consortium members are very different from one another. A well-established and important criterion for Five Colleges joint efforts is that, for any given project, only institutions that stand to benefit need collaborate. In some cases, like the joint insurance and risk management program, the University of Massachusetts participates in a systemwide program and therefore could not join with the private colleges in this project. In others, such as the shared benefits programs, some institutions' individual cost structures may not make a combined program economically beneficial. Should those economies change, opportunities always exist for joining the combined program at a later stage. For institutions to enter willingly and wholeheartedly into joint efforts, they must be able to see current or future benefits over individual efforts. Maintaining flexibility while joint programs are created ultimately strengthens the overall collaboration.

As individual institutions, Five Colleges members are discovering the need to improve internal group processes to respond effectively to a rapidly changing environment. In consortia, effective group processes are fundamental to achieving successful collaboration. As important on a different level is building among consortium members what Hampshire College President and current Five Colleges President Gregory Prince calls a "climate of cooperation." Even in a cooperative effort as long-standing as Five Colleges, tremendous inertia remains. Individual institutions must repeatedly remind themselves to think about undertaking projects together before setting about doing it individually. Five Colleges will have achieved an important paradigm shift when its members automatically turn to the group first to see if something can be done together rather than instinctively going their separate institutional ways.

In an environment that demands increasingly rapid change, how responsive the group can be to those external demands for change is an issue that is always close to the surface. Change can be both more difficult and easier for a consortium than for an individual institu-

tion. The greater difficulties are obvious and some have been alluded
to earlier in this chapter: more players to bring into agreement, different cultures to reconcile, and multiple communities of constitu-
ent groups to convince. The ways in which change is easier are more
subtle. Once change is clearly identified as a goal, a group approach
allows each institution's strengths and many more individuals' talents to be pooled toward the best possible outcome. Options that
would be impossible for a single institution to achieve become realis-
tic for the group. And even with projects that are possible for each
institution individually, a single, combined outcome is likely to be a
superior product because it benefits from the best thinking of a larger
group of talented people.

One characteristic of existing consortia that may become less
important in the future is geographic proximity. The nearness of each
campus to the others has certainly been a critical success factor for
Five Colleges in allowing students and faculty easy access to all campuses and in facilitating the regular and inexpensive meeting of working groups. However, as technology changes the implications of
physical distance, many new kinds of collaborative work become not
only possible, but efficient as well. Even consortium members in close
proximity will be able to take advantage of new applications such as
on-line laboratory experiments that can be observed or even actively
attended by students with their individual computers on their various home campuses. Distance learning in all its aspects has powerful
implications for consortia.

Another issue facing consortia, which is also rooted in universities and systems, is that of centralization versus decentralization. And
the questions to be asked are very much the same: How is the program or service most effectively delivered? Where are the economies
of scale and are they offset by lack of fit with the users? How is bureaucracy avoided? One might argue that much of the work in combining operations at a consortial level flies in the face of many of the
efforts at universities and systems to become more effective by decentralizing operations. However, the continuum between providing
every program and service centrally and duplicating every program
and service on each campus is exceedingly wide. Much can be learned
from the efforts of large institutions and university systems as they
move along this continuum. For institutions without a history of collaboration in any form, there is much that can effectively be shared
without approaching the level of the most decentralized of the uni-

versities. There is no one right place to be on this continuum, but a middle ground exists within which many universities, systems, and consortia can comfortably fit.

As consortia begin to combine operations, several models become available for organizing this new work. Some consortia develop a central services arm of the consortium that houses and oversees the joint operations. Others parcel out the shared staff among the member campuses, with oversight through a consortial committee or consortium office. For consortia without central staffing, campuses can contract or share with one another, with some providing services to other campuses as well as their own. Whichever model or combination of models emerges, a consortium will be successful to the extent that it is built on a foundation of shared goals, strong communications, and planning linkages.

Conclusion

The inevitable conversation within consortia is how far cooperative efforts can or should go. A number of operations can readily be combined—at least in theory. However, as soon as serious investigation is done on the actual combining of operations, a fundamental question emerges: At what point does the combination begin to encroach into areas that are culturally specific or give identity to an individual institution? What about combined residence programs or career services offices or academic advising? What about a single financial office or shared endowment management? If a few academic departments can be combined, why not all of them? At what point in the process does the institutional distinctiveness of consortium members begin to blur?

Put differently, is a consortium an intermediate step down the road to combination? For some institutions, the answer may be yes. For most institutions, however, consortia are an end in themselves— a means of developing a competitive edge in an extremely competitive market. The tension between reaping the benefits—in both cost reduction and programmatic richness—of cooperation and blurring the boundaries between institutions persists at each stage of consortial effort. What the institution perceives as its boundaries changes over time as group efforts become more comfortable and their value becomes more apparent. However, at the stage of truly joint operations, the tension becomes much more starkly focused. This tension is natural, since the progression of collaborative efforts would inevitably lead to a single combined operation were there not more powerful reasons to keep some group of core functions separate. Although Five Colleges is far from this point, its members will likely eventually reach a rough equilibrium between what is usefully done together and what must remain separate. This new relationship will provide the best of both worlds—the ability to take maximum advantage of collaboration, which in turn frees the resources for each institution to polish its special and distinctive qualities.

Rethinking the Academy's Administrative Structure

3

Jillinda J. Kidwell
David O'Brien

This chapter is reprinted with permission from Reinventing the University: Managing and Financing Institutions of Higher Education *edited by Sandra L. Johnson and Sean C. Rush, Coopers & Lybrand L.L.P. Published by John Wiley & Sons, Inc., copyright 1994.*

The Growth of Administration Inefficiency

For well over two centuries, including the most recent 40 years of extraordinary post–World War II growth, the basic *academic* organizational structure of U.S. higher education has remained essentially unchanged. Academic endeavors continue to function, with notable success, through a loosely coupled system of individual faculty interacting within intellectual disciplines organized into academic programs, divisions, departments, schools, colleges, and universities.

For most of its long history, a recognizable *administrative* support organization for an institution's academic endeavors has been notably absent. In the past 20 years, however, administrative support organizations have emerged as a significant component in most institutions, and administrative operations are an increasingly expensive portion of the institutional budget.

Understanding Administrative Growth

Administrative resources within academia have traditionally been aligned as directly as possible in support of faculty activities. The long-held principles of academic freedom grant each faculty member an enormous degree of latitude over the direction and content of their academic pursuits. Under this guiding principle, as the business of academia has grown, so has the amount of administrative resources allocated and controlled at the faculty level. The need to manage dramatically increasing amounts of programmatically controlled academic resources has produced increasingly large administrative support groups attached to individual faculty and program groups, to divisional and department chairs, and to school deans. Similar specialized administrative groups support university offices under the direction of provosts, vice presidents, and presidents. Over time, bureaucratic expansion has resulted in a lack of clarity in the current business model, that is, in the distribution of responsibility, authority, and workload among the university, its school, and its departments.

Institutions of higher education now conduct their critical and complicated administrative operations through a hierarchical organizational structure that directly parallels, and is appended to, its fundamental, underlying academic structure. Since ultimate institutional accountability is held centrally and most resource and spending authority is delegated locally (to faculty), seemingly reasonable operational control objectives have produced elaborate administrative processes that tend to wind their way up through successive layers of administrative oversight groups until, at a sufficiently high level of the organization, approval is given and the desired action takes place.

Departmental Process Navigators and Central Specialists

Process Navigators. These labyrinthine processes have gradually required a change in academic departmental administrative structures. The faculty secretaries of old have given rise to local administrative assistants, or *process navigators,* on whom the faculty rely to move things through (or around) the administrative system. Process navigators provide to the faculty their only safe, reliable, and responsive access to byzantine university administrative systems. They are administrative generalists who know enough about all the university administrative systems to get the paperwork started and keep it moving. Whether it is a research proposal submission, a travel reimbursement, a simple equipment purchase, or a personnel requisition, the road to administrative approval begins at the door of the process navigator.

If the paperwork is not managed by a process navigator and is left to wend its own way through the university process, the results are disastrous. In the hiring process, for example, the faculty process navigator knows *who* to contact in central employment and *when* to contact them to get the posting date retroactively dated, thereby cutting nearly two weeks off the posting time (or even better, how to waive out of the posting period altogether). The ultimate triumph of a process navigator is to exceed the expectations of the faculty member and develop an expedient work-around process that gets the job done. Process navigators are ferociously loyal to faculty and will go to whatever lengths are necessary to shepherd the paperwork through the system and keep the frustrations and inefficiencies of the system away from their employers. The final outcome of this business model is that process navigators need departmental resources to build "shadow systems," maintain logs, manage databases that track the progress of paperwork, or provide access to up-to-date management information to make the process itself invisible to the faculty member or department chair.

Central Specialists. The road process navigators must travel leads through numerous "central" offices, corresponding to the traditional hierarchy of the academic organization, and across the desks of administrators who specialize in specific administrative areas, such as sponsored projects, travel reimbursement, capital equipment, or personnel. As loyal as the local administrators are to their faculty, *central specialists* are equally loyal and committed to their bosses. Central specialists are defined by their ability to protect the university's administrative/control interests within their particular areas of expertise. Consequently, their paperwork reviews more often than not result in redirection of the paperwork back down the road to unsuspecting faculty and their process navigators for additional information or corrections. For the local process navigator the process proceeds with two steps forward and one step back, until the end of the road is eventually reached. Throughout it all, process navigators have two purposes: to get to the end of the road as quickly as possible and not to burden faculty with their problems in getting there.

In the past several years, attempts have been made to reduce the high costs associated with this business model. Central university administrators have been stymied in their attempts to "fix" their processes because they exert control over—or "own"—a relatively small portion of the administrative activities that comprise the end-to-end process. Typically, only 20 percent of the overall process is under the control of most central university offices. The remaining process activities are controlled by the dean's office staff, academic departmental chairs, or individual faculty members.

The Business Case for Change

Reducing the costs built into its complicated hierarchy is one of the most significant challenges facing U.S. higher education today. The task of rationalizing the costs of administration in light of a dramatically shifting, underlying economic picture is daunting. The past years of administrative growth have been fueled, in large part, through a fortuitous combination of factors, including a robust national economy, high interest rates, strong federal investments in cost-reimbursed basic research, and a steadily expanding and cost-reimbursed national healthcare agenda that has funded growth in medical schools.

However, beginning as early as the mid-1980s, planners in higher education began to raise concerns about the potential dampening of these fundamental growth factors. The preceding decades of growth had produced an even more rapidly expanding community of academics forced to compete ever more aggressively for smaller pieces of the higher education pie. As interest rates began to come down, so did expendable earnings from institutional endowments. Student tolerances for double-digit inflation in tuition and fees have similarly decreased with declining interest rates. The growth in federal support of research has begun to flatten (in constant-dollar spending) and become refocused on direct costs at the expense of institutional overhead cost, a trend that was most recently reflected in the capping of administrative costs recoverable from federally sponsored research. A slower economy has significantly constrained state and local funding available for public higher education. Tax code changes have similarly dampened philanthropic support to private higher education. For institutions involved in healthcare delivery, the continuing shift from cost-reimbursed to capitated healthcare systems, both federally funded and private, have eroded a significant source of support to academic programs.

The economic picture for higher education in the 1990s differs in almost every way from that which supported the past decades of programmatic and administrative growth. The administrative organization which emerged from that period was largely unplanned and it remains unchallenged. It is characterized by administrative processes that are so interwoven into the fabric of academic departmental administration as to be nearly inseparable. The new economic realities confronting higher education require a serious rethinking of the way that work is done, the way it is organized, and the systems needed to support the academic enterprise. To develop successfully a new business model appropriate to the economics of the future, this rethinking needs to question the academic departmental base as the underlying condition for the delivery of administrative support services.

The Re-engineered Organization

Several years ago, administrators responded to the cost crisis as if it was a temporary problem and financial resources would ultimately return to their previous levels, enabling them to spring forward to even higher levels of administrative support. Their early response to budget imbalances was to implement across-the-board cost-cutting measures or to freeze administrative budgets. Each of these approaches may have balanced the budget temporarily but did little to provide long-term budget relief. These approaches produced unsatisfactory results because administrative work did not go away. Instead, fewer staff remained and were required to do more with reduced resources. Although some forward thinking institutions implemented innovative strategies in response to the cost crisis, such as total quality management (TQM) initiatives, the results have been incremental. To achieve the systemic changes needed in higher education today requires more dramatic approaches than TQM and other traditional measures.

As evidence mounts that the cost crisis is long term and structural in nature, more and more institutions are seeking ways to initiate radical organizational restructuring. The current administrative hierarchical organization requires more than tinkering around the margins. To accomplish change of the magnitude required in administrative structures today, colleges and universities need to question the underlying assumptions regarding the structure of administrative tasks. The outcome of this questioning should lead to organizational restructuring, management delayering, employee empowerment, and a culture that is less bureaucratic. Those who embark on this road need to be prepared to restructure their business services and administrative operations radically, even to the point of giving up certain responsibilities, taking on new responsibilities,

or collaborating in heretofore unheard of ways (e.g., "hub" structures to provide administrative services to a group of three or more
departments).

The Corporate Experience

Death of the Corporate Hierarchy. Many corporations have faced
and overcome the challenges currently confronting higher
education. An army of writers is declaring the death of corporate
bureaucracy. The U.S. corporate structure—defined by complex organizations, hierarchical chains of command, narrowly defined roles
and responsibilities, numerous layers of management, and excessive division of labor is considered a superfluous artifact of a by-
gone era that is becoming increasingly irrelevant in today's
demanding environment. According to re-engineering gurus Hammer and Champy:

> Advanced technologies, the disappearance of boundaries between
> national markets, and the altered expectations of customers who
> now have more choices than ever before have combined to make
> the goals, methods, and basic organizing principles of the classical
> American corporation sadly obsolete. Renewing their competitive
> capabilities isn't an issue of getting people in these companies to
> work harder, but of learning to work differently. This means that
> companies and their employees must unlearn many of the prin-
> ciples and techniques that brought them success for so long.[1]

In his book *The Rebirth of the Corporation,* D. Quinn Mills disdains
the traditional hierarchy and considers it a threat to our economic
survival. He proclaims:

> The traditional hierarchical structure of our companies is more than
> just a system that has outlived its usefulness—it is a clear and present
> danger to the economic welfare of all of us . . . .
>   Perhaps in the past companies needed to be organized as if they
> were old-time military units. People were poorly educated and re-
> quired precise direction. They were reluctant to work and poorly
> self-disciplined, so they needed close supervision. Because commu-
> nications were slow and information difficult to obtain, many people
> were needed to collect information and prepare reports for top
> executives. The result was a pyramid of supervision managers who

kept business humming and rewarded themselves with good salaries and high status.[2]

Emergence of a New Way of Work. Today's corporate re-engineers are taking apart current hierarchical business models and are developing in their stead *process-oriented* organization structures. Although some corporations have re-engineered superficially, at other corporations, corporate structures are being turned on their sides and upside down. Customers who were previously viewed as the downstream receivers of the output of the organization are moving upstream to the front end of the process to help define product requirements. Organizational boundaries are blurring and the edges of the corporation are merging with suppliers, becoming boundaryless organizations.

People in these organizations are adopting new ways of work. As they become focused on the needs and desires of their customers and are empowered to design responsive systems, their need for a traditional boss wanes. As the end-to-end process is organized into a single unit, narrow bands of specialization vanish and staff are responsible for the overall performance of the process and the results it delivers to customers. Ultimately, employees are organized as self-managed process teams that no longer rely on the directives of a middle manager to inform their daily, monthly, or annual activities. Concomitant with this change, old functional departments disappear, managers become more like coaches, and the traditional hierarchy begins to flatten. Ultimately, as the people who deliver the process implement a re-engineered process and provide service that exceeds expectations, the need for process navigators evaporates. If an institution is committed to organizational change, the cost to deliver service is reduced dramatically.

Gifford and Elizabeth Pinchot explain this new way of work in compelling terms. They believe that bureaucracies are giving way to the rise of an intelligent organization. Employees in these new organizations

> . . . put their heads together to milk opportunities, co-create products and services, find and solve problems. They "get in over their heads" and help each other emerge with stronger skills and a bit more wisdom. Employees run their areas like small businesses, service their internal and external customers with care and work with

others across the organization to make sure the whole system is going well. Everyone, not just the people at the top, is exercising his
or her intelligence and responsibility at work.[3]

The Applicability of Re-engineering to Higher Education

The Pinchots' description of the emerging work system for the
corporate sector sounds almost too good to be true. It may seem
difficult to achieve in the higher education sector. It is sometimes
hard to imagine that staff will be able produce the results promised
by re-engineering. Higher education's elaborate system of controls,
checks, and balances does not lend itself readily to the creation of an
empowered workforce. Approvals are required because there are no
consequences for abuses to the system. Numerous signatures create
the illusion of control.

Higher education's reliance on numerous signatures also leads
to the creation of tracking systems to monitor the process. Most processes are characterized by a series of handoffs and black holes. Tracking the transaction becomes an activity in its own right. Staff members
develop systems so they are able to respond to queries regarding the
status of the transaction and assure the caller that their small piece of
the activity is done and they have sent the paperwork on its way.

It is resoundingly apparent that *radical,* systemic change is needed
in higher education's underlying processes to overcome the built-in
inefficiencies of the processes and to achieve the vision described by
the Pinchots and other proponents of re-engineering. But process
change in not enough. The current culture of mistrust and control
leads to "checkers" checking "checkers" and to a system that rewards
the creation of work-around processes. This culture is a strong im-
pediment to change.

To realize the results of process re-engineering, accompanying
changes are required in the systems, organization structures, cultures,
and values that undergird higher education's current business model.
New technology that provides decision-making information to the
person closest to the customer is needed. Expert systems that contain simple rules for choosing options can tell faculty and staff imme-
diately what to do rather than taking hours paging through various
manuals and policy books or turning to central specialists to find the
answer.

Finally, higher education's underlying management values need
to change before its workforce has the luxury to operate in the man-

ner described by the Pinchots. Classification systems need to become less restrictive, and people working in self-directed teams need new methods of feedback in their performance evaluations. Abuses require consequences. Exceptional work needs to be rewarded.

The Re-engineering Process: An Overview

The new corporate organization is customer driven, results focused, and performance based. Importantly, the new organization will shift its focus from a functional or "vertical" orientation to a process view and will "go horizontal." Processes that have been fragmented across several departments will be restructured into a cohesive whole and will be designed to provide services to end customers in the most cost-effective manner.

This new *process mantra* is the basis of re-engineering and has transformed many organizational structures into process-based organizations. Re-engineering therefore begins with the identification of an institution's processes. A process is a series of linked activities in which an input is transformed into an output and a tangible product is delivered to an external customer.

But processes are hard to define. Rigorous application of Adam Smith's principles of division of labor has built a hierarchical structure in which excessive departmentalization makes it nearly impossible to identify the end-to-end process. The beginning of the process often has no connection to its end. Because most processes are characterized by handoffs among numerous departments and obscured by complicated work steps, many organizations spend days simply defining their processes.

Process definition begins with the identification of an organization's outputs and the identification of the external customer to whom those outputs are delivered. In higher education, attaining agreement on the definition of the institution's customer often proves to be an arduous task. For some institutions, even the mention of the word *customer* is distasteful because it connotes a businesslike attitude that many college and university faculty and administrators abhor.

This reluctance to accept the existence of an external customer and the rejection of the idea that an institution produces measurable outputs and products is an obstacle to higher education's re-engineering efforts. For example, a reengineering team that fails to define its customers correctly will—by default—fail to define the

university's core processes correctly. Re-engineering teams that abdi-
cate their responsibility and do not own up to the customer definition task will be hampered in their re-engineering efforts. For
example, a team that agrees to an amorphous customer definition,
such as the state's taxpayers or the general public, will find it difficult
to define the product that is delivered to the customer or the process
that creates the product. Unless accurate definitions of customers
and outputs are achieved, defining processes and creating an institutional process map is nearly impossible.

Despite the difficulties in defining an institution's processes, it *is*
an approach that is applicable to colleges and universities and provides interesting results, as described in the example later in this
chapter.

Evaluating and Fixing Processes

Once an institution's processes have been defined, they can be
evaluated according to their degree of criticality to its mission. A process framework allows an institution to evaluate its processes along a
scale of salience, that is: How central are they to the mission and
competitive advantage of the institution? The degree of saliency indicates the value an institution's processes deliver. In deciding what
to re-engineer, an institution can use process saliency to help determine the amount of investment they intend to make in reinventing
the process. Investments should be made to improve the institution's
most value-creating processes. Investment in other processes should
not exceed the value they provide the institution. Processes can be
categorized as core and non-core. Core processes can be further segmented into identity and priority processes. Likewise, non-core processes can be further segmented into background and mandated
processes.[4] These are defined as:

1. An *identity* process is what an institution stands for, "who" it is,
    and how customers think about it. The institution's vision, mis-
    sion, values, priorities, and sense of shared culture all relate to its
    identity processes. This category of processes must be consciously
    maintained as an asset and strategically positioned to avoid be-
    coming a liability.
2. *Priority* processes are important elements of an institution's busi-
    ness and link directly to and support its identity processes. These

processes make a material difference in the ability of an institution to achieve a leadership position in its identity processes.

3. *Background* processes are part of what an institution does but do not directly support its identity processes. As such, background processes should not consume undue time, resources, or attention, nor divert critical resources away from the institution's identity and priority processes. Interestingly, background processes tend to harbor the most waste. As such, re-engineering efforts are often centered around ways in which to reduce costs for background processes at the lowest investment possible.

4. *Mandated* processes are performed only because the government or other external agencies impose them on an institution. Regulation is the major source of such processes, which rarely adds economic value. Care should be taken to reduce the amount of effort and expense expended on these processes and yet comply adequately with regulation.

Not all processes should be re-engineered. As re-engineering teams begin the task of evaluating an institution's processes and designing new ones, they should initially ask hard questions designed to identify processes for elimination or outsourcing. Teams should challenge the status quo by asking whether the service needs to be done at all. If not, it should be eliminated. In these times of financial stringency, institutions should cut back (if not cut out) "nice to have" but nonessential services.

If the activity or service is essential but not an identity or priority process, can it be outsourced? This requires looking beyond traditionally outsourced services such as bookstores and dining services and examining whether services such as physical plant, payroll, human resources, audit, computing, security, "back office processing," and a host of other activities are suitable candidates for outsourcing. According to a recent *Business Week* article:

> Hundreds of big companies have outsourced noncore operations: Continental Bank Corp. has contracted its legal, audit, cafeteria, and mailroom operations to outside companies. In September, American Airlines Inc. announced it would do the same with customer service jobs at 30 airports.... Outsourcing can work wonders for the bottom line: So-called contingent workers get pay comparable to full-time staffs, but without benefits that typically add 40% to labor costs. A contingent workforce, too, is more flexible: When

business sags, the temps go first. Blue Cross/Blue Shield of Rhode Island cut its workforce by 40% over five years without laying off a single full timer.[5]

If the essential activity or service cannot or should not be outsourced, how can it be made more cost-effective, customer responsive, and efficient? For example, can redundant administrative work taking place in a multitude of departments be "in-sourced" to a process team to provide end-to-end process service while increasing timeliness and service delivery? Can the process be completely automated using advanced technology? Can the organizational model be restructured by creating a single customer service desk for students that handles registration, housing, service privileges (e.g., library card), dining, financial aid, and other essential student services? Is it possible to design a hybrid process in which a central organization sets standards and provides necessary infrastructure, yet which is decentralized to the end user?

There are numerous types of process solutions; one size does not fit all. Each institution will make unique decisions based on its mission, values, and the degree of supporting technology that exists. Importantly, the decision regarding which solutions are needed to fix the process begin by defining the customer and determining how the process creates value for the customer.

Higher Education's Process Map

Before processes can be redesigned, they need to be defined and the degree to which they are interrelated must be understood. One of the key tools of re-engineering is the creation of a high-level business process map. According to Hammer and Champy:

> Process maps don't require months of work to construct; several weeks is the norm. But this task does induce headaches, because it requires people to think across the organizational grain. It's not a picture of the organization, which is what people are used to seeing and drawing, but a depiction of the work that is being done. When it's finished, the process map should not surprise anyone. In fact, people may wonder why drawing it took as long as it did, since the finished map will be so easy to understand, even obvious. "Of course," people should say, "that's just a model of what we do around here."[6]

To create the map, it is necessary to identify the outputs created by the institution's core processes and define the customers to whom these outputs are delivered. The map, by definition, does not show departments, but rather, shows how work is done in the organization. Because processes have been obscured by organizational structures, employees often have a difficult time creating the first process map. The first step is to ignore department, college, or divisional reporting relationships and think about the processes that define the organization.

Most colleges and universities are able to distill their identify and priority processes into five to ten core processes. The way in which an institution implements each of these processes helps establish its reputation in the academic community. These core identity and priority processes are listed in figure 3-1. Their distinct relationships to each other are expressed in a high-level process map in figure 3-2 and described in the next paragraph.

Although the reputation of an institution is based on a number of factors, its implementation of its core processes contribute directly to and affect its reputation. How does this happen? One of higher education's core processes is its ability to create and sustain a dynamic and compelling intellectual community. The establishment of that community—accomplished by its strategic planning and budget setting processes—is one of the primary assets that enable an institution to attract and retain faculty. Subsequently, these faculty members generate knowledge through research, educate students, and provide community service. Their teaching, research, and service activities produce distinct and measurable products (outputs) to the institution's customers, including the business community that employs its students, federal agencies that fund its research, patients that receive medical care, and community members that receive direct service, to name a few. Finally, customer satisfaction levels, changing customer needs, and the emergence of new customers inform its strategic planning process.

Each of the processes on the high-level process map in figure 3-2 explode to create detailed maps of the corresponding subprocesses (figure 3-3). These detailed subprocess maps can be blown up even further to identify the tasks required by each person in each department to complete the process.

The high-level process map provides a framework in which to discuss transforming higher education because it shows how processes

Figure 3-1: Activity Dictionary — Higher Education's Five Identity Processes

Conduct strategic planning and allocate resources to create, sustain, and revise the institutional intellectual community / environment.

Assess environment. Environmental scanning to determine future academic and research needs. Communicating with external customers. Identify opportunities and threats.

Set academic vision and priorities. Based on the environmental scan and review of the institution's strengths and weaknesses, develop a vision for the future and identify priorities.

Establish/revise academic structure. Implement change to the academic structure of the institution, add/eliminate programs, schools, etc.

Formulate budgeting strategy and monitor results. Create strategic and operational plans departmentally, schoolwide, and campus-wide. Assess projections versus actual activities, prepare management reports, evaluate performance.

Output: The output of these sets of planning and budgeting activities is the creation of an intellectual community by which an institution attracts and retains its faculty.

Manage faculty resources.

Recruit faculty and retain faculty.
Implement promotion and tenure process.

Generate new knowledge.

Through the conduct of research, faculty generate new knowledge. See figure 3-3 for a list of the subprocesses that comprise this core process.

Educate students.

Provide services to local, state, and national communities.

Figure 3-2: Higher Education's Process Map

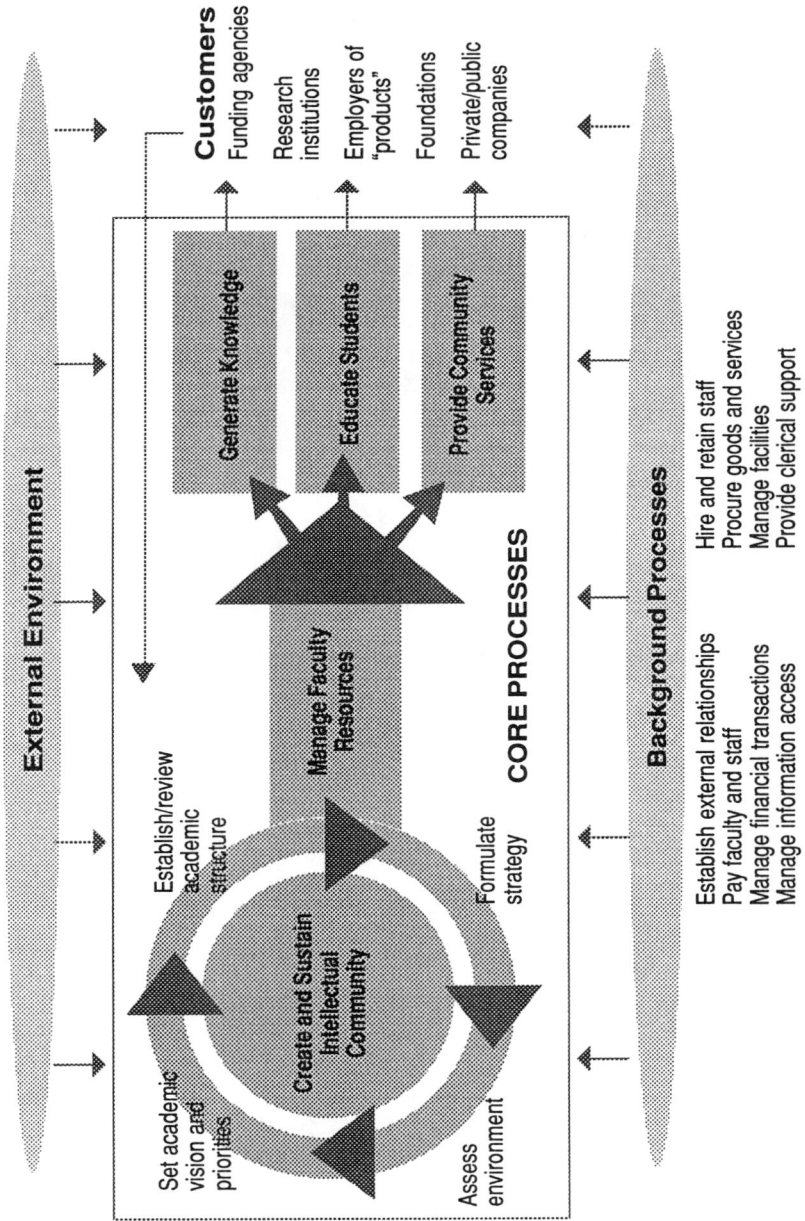

Customers
- Funding agencies
- Research institutions
- Employers of "products"
- Foundations
- Private/public companies

External Environment

Generate Knowledge

Educate Students

Provide Community Services

Manage Faculty Resources

CORE PROCESSES

Establish/review academic structure

Create and Sustain Intellectual Community

Set academic vision and priorities

Formulate strategy

Assess environment

Background Processes
- Hire and retain staff
- Procure goods and services
- Manage facilities
- Provide clerical support
- Establish external relationships
- Pay faculty and staff
- Manage financial transactions
- Manage information access

Figure 3-3: Subprocess Map for Knowledge Generation Process

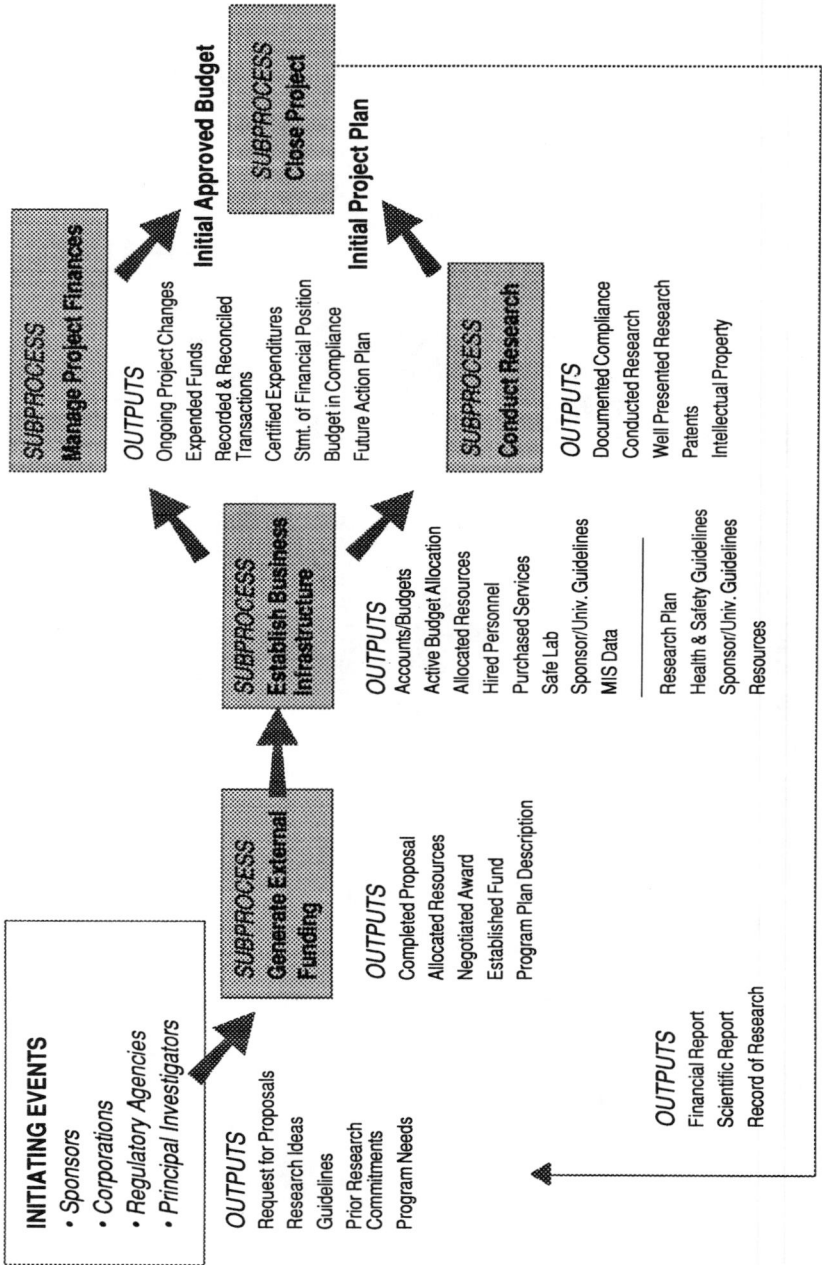

link to and support the institution. Importantly, the map depicts the way in which work is done. By re-engineering processes and reorganizing around the way in which work is done, higher education can create new organizational structures that ignore traditional hierarchical boundaries and follow the horizontal nature of work.

This process philosophy formed the basis for discussion of the Stanford University School of Medicine study. The Stanford University School of Medicine situation provides a microcosm of what is happening in higher education today. The school has experienced phenomenal growth but is in the midst of a significant cost crisis. In 1994 a representative group of the school's staff began to explore ways to deal with its budget crisis. The group evaluated traditional cost-saving strategies and rejected them. Their research led them to conclude that radical restructuring of administrative support was the only valid response to the budget problem.

The Stanford University School of Medicine Experience

In 1961–1962 the Stanford University School of Medicine reported a total consolidated budget of just under $7.1 million. At that time, the school consisted of 118 faculty members supported by 72 administrative staff. Of these staff, nearly 80 percent were faculty and departmental secretaries. Consequently, in 1961–1962, less than $500,000 was budgeted for administrative staff throughout the school. This amounted to less than 6 percent of the school's total spending and just 4 percent of all department spending. The entire central administration of the school consisted of three administrative deans and seven support staff.

By 1991–1992, although Stanford's School of Medicine faculty size had increased by nearly 400 percent over its 1961–1962 size, to 571 faculty, its consolidated budget had grown to a total of $231.2 million (a constant dollar increase of over 600 percent). This expanded enterprise was supported with a 1,000 percent increase in administrative staff, now totaling 835 people in 76 different job types, and a 1,700 percent (constant dollar) increase in total administrative costs. Secretaries (although budgeted within five different job grades) comprised just 20 percent of the administrative workforce. The predominate departmental job groups are now administrative assistants, office assistants, and accountants. Administrative costs now consume nearly 15 percent of all school spending and over 25 percent of departmental spending. The rise in faculty process navigators has produced a constant-dollar increase of over 300 percent in departmental administrative costs per faculty member.

Despite a conventionally organized, well-developed, well-funded, and well-staffed administration supported with all the latest advances in automated administrative systems, in 1990, a series of procedural and accounting problems came to light at Stanford University which called into question the integrity of the cost-accounting data supporting the university's sponsored research indirect cost rate. As a result, the federal government unexpectedly and retroactively reduced the university's effective indirect cost rate by over 30 percent, which at the Stanford School of Medicine resulted in an immediate and sustained loss of some $1 million in budgeted unrestricted annual income. This represented a loss of nearly 20 percent of the support behind the school's general funds.

Although it had recently undertaken a downsizing effort in response to more subtle changes in its financial forecasts, the school's administration responded to the lost indirect cost recoveries with a immediate 5 percent reduction in central administrative staff, followed shortly thereafter by an across-the-board 7 percent reduction in general funds allocations to academic departments, a one-time salary freeze reductions in planned faculty billet increases, and an additional 6 percent reduction in central administrative units. Combined with other adjustments in the school's financial plans and reserves management practices, by 1993 these actions left the school with a continuing base budget shortfall of about $2 million.

At the request of the school's dean, a group of departmental and central administrators convened to study the school's administrative costs and to advise the dean on options for reducing costs further to achieve a balanced budget. In addition to continuing to pursue conventional downsizing approaches and exploring opportunities for reducing costs through TQM-type approaches, this study included an assessment of the applicability of business process re-engineering (BPR) approaches to administrative restructuring at the School of Medicine. The results of the study have proven to be invaluable in helping the school's academic and administrative leaders to better understand the limitations of continuing with their prevailing model and to identify the risks and opportunities.

The School's Process Map

The hierarchy of activities and taxonomy of administrative processes presented earlier provided a unifying framework for studying the School of Medicine's administrative costs and structure. Stanford's study began with the development of a process map of the School of Medicine activities. Traditional administrative inventories usually ask the question, "What do we do?" and tend to produce effort measures within the existing organizational chart. A high-level process-based view of the school was produced by repeatedly asking the question, "To what end do we do what we do?" and yielded a unique view of the critical outputs of the school. The school's data indicated that between 525 and 590 fulltime equivalents (FTEs) of staff effort was expended in administrative tasks. These FTEs cost the school between $30 million and $35 million. Despite the relative importance of the priority processes to the success of the school's academic mission, nearly three-fourths of the FTEs and two-thirds of the staff costs were attributable to the administration of background processes. In figure 3-4 these processes are depicted on a process map to indicate how each process links to and supports other processes and to show the output to the school's customers. It also shows the costs (in millions of dollars) of the school's administrative activities.

Perceptions of the School's Administrative Processes

Focus groups representing the recipients (customers) of the schools administrative efforts indicated a high degree of customer dissatisfaction with the performance of nearly all of the school's administrative processes. The faculty's confidence in the administration's value, ability, and willingness to get things done decreased in direct correlation to the distance at which the process activity took place from their own offices. From the faculty's perspective, the most valuable participant in the process was their local administrator. The only way to get anything done was to rely on their local administrator—the process navigator—as a go-between, bridging the gulf between their academic program needs and an unfathomable and unresponsive administrative bureaucracy.

Local administrators clearly viewed faculty as their customers and expressed their frustrations with this go-between role and the extraordinary effort expended in meeting the demands of faculty. Faculty

Figure 3-4: Stanford University School of Medicine's Process Map

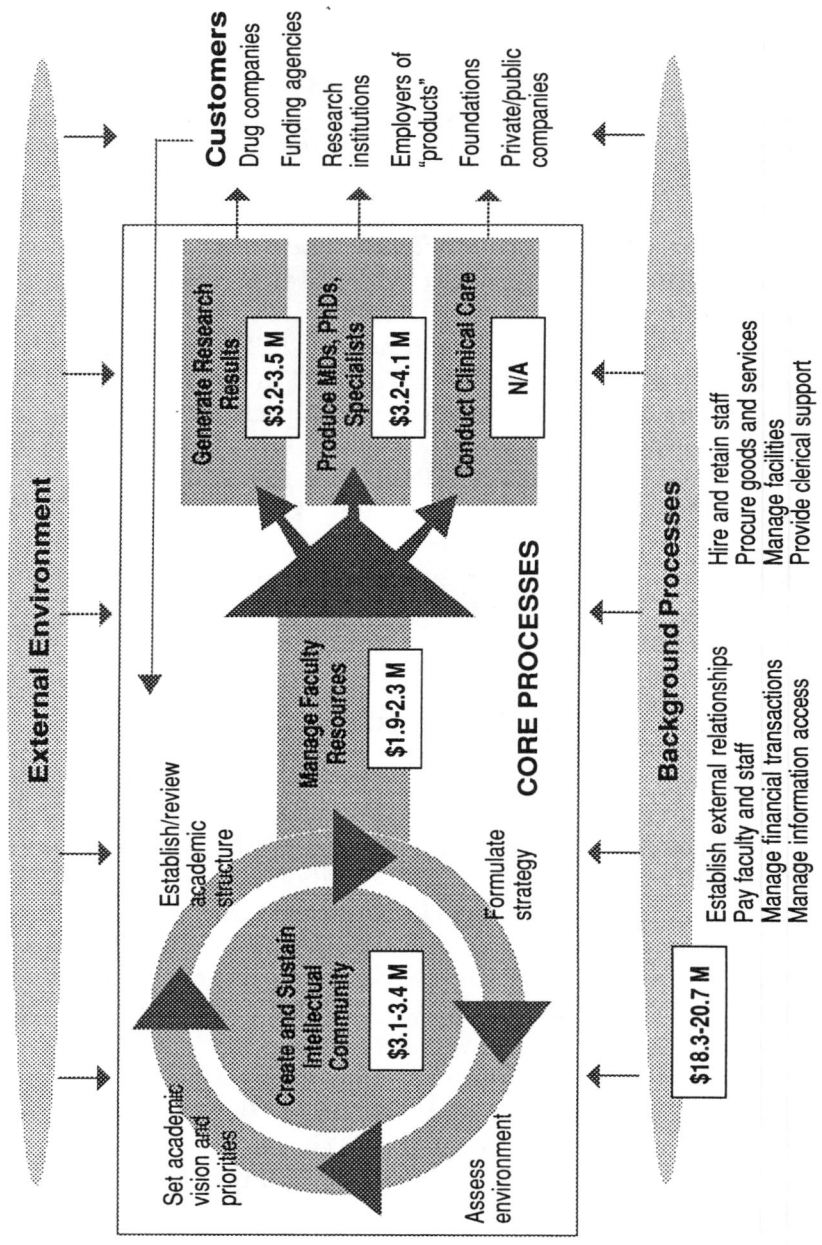

External Environment

Customers
- Drug companies
- Funding agencies
- Research institutions
- Employers of "products"
- Foundations
- Private/public companies

Generate Research Results — $3.2-3.5 M

Produce MDs, PhDs, Specialists — $3.2-4.1 M

Conduct Clinical Care — N/A

CORE PROCESSES

Manage Faculty Resources — $1.9-2.3 M

Establish/review academic structure

Formulate strategy

Create and Sustain Intellectual Community — $3.1-3.4 M

Set academic vision and priorities

Assess environment

Background Processes
- Hire and retain staff
- Procure goods and services
- Manage facilities
- Provide clerical support
- Establish external relationships
- Pay faculty and staff
- Manage financial transactions
- Manage information access

$18.3-20.7 M

and their local administrators expressed a distrust of the motives and abilities of central medical school administration and suggested that if they could simply be left to do their jobs, things would run just fine. Local administrators evidenced a particular pride in the private shadow systems they developed to support their work in ways in which the official university systems could not. They frequently measured their successes by heroic abilities at shortcutting the university's processes, often their knowledge of key persons at critical steps in the process. "Process busting" was a skill valued by faculty and an activity from which administrators derived professional pride.

Focus groups representing the providers of central medical school administrative services generally saw the university or external agencies as their customers. They expressed great frustration with the attitudes and capabilities of the faculty and their local administrators. They felt that if the faculty and staff would just learn the university's policies and procedures, the jobs in the medical school's central offices would be made much easier. While these central administrators acknowledged their effect on the pace of administration and the frustrations expressed by the local staff as a result of their prolonged reviews and frequent returns of work, they consistently rated the quality of their work as "high." This is an understandable difference in perception from the faculty view since central administrators did not see the faculty and local administrators as their customers.

In all the focus groups, individuals expressed a clear understanding of their specific jobs. They knew in infinite detail their particular pieces of processes that usually began and ended elsewhere in the institution. They did not, however, express a sense of ownership of the overall conduct of any process. From a process view, the School of Medicine's administration consisted of a vast array of individuals all working very hard at their assigned tasks, with little or no understanding or ownership of their contributory role within the larger processes that define the success of the school.

Implications of Administrative Fragmentation

Detailed staff effort data were collected and analyzed by the School of Medicine re-engineering team. They helped express the administrative effort and costs of the school in light of the processes involved. Reinforcing the findings of the focus groups, the data gathered indicated a great deal of process fragmentation within the School of

Medicine. Within an organizational unit (i.e., a division or a department) numerous individual staff members were involved in the various phases of the processes. Also, staff from across all levels of the organization indicated participation in the process.

Not surprising, then, were the data indicating a similarly high degree of position fragmentation with the school's processes. Position fragmentation is a measure of the number of people required to yield a full FTE of administrative effort within a process area. The lower the ratio, the better. Figure 3-5 shows a sample process fragmentation table. At the School of Medicine, position fragmentation ratios ranged from a low of 1.75 (recruiting M.D. and Ph.D. students) to a high of 10.37 (research project closeout). Across all processes the school averaged a fragmentation ratio of 1.57. Within its priority processes, however, the ratios were 2.66 (educating students), 3.42 (establishing vision and recruiting and retaining faculty), and 3.81 (generating research results).

These ratios were a concern for two significant reasons. First, they indicate that even within the priority areas so critical to the success of the school, the average administrator was only spending one-fourth to one third of his or her time "doing" the priority process. The rest of their time was spent in largely administrative tasks outside a particular priority process area.

The second reason for concern was the implication of the ratios on the potential for successful sustained downsizing efforts. Traditional downsizing efforts were not possible because across-the-board cost cuts do not eliminate administrative work. Similarly, reducing administrative costs by implementing incremental process improvement (TQM) did not offer the prospect of sustained cost savings. Although minor process change can improve performance, it is impossible to translate those efficiency improvements into reduced staff costs. This is because radical improvement in work flows in at least three or four processes is required to achieve significant staff reductions. The school's data showed that efforts to achieve cost savings from incremental process improvement in a highly fragmented work environment is hindered by the fact that these improvements usually affect only a portion of a person's job.

It became increasingly apparent that without dramatic changes in work flow and organization, the school would not be able to achieve the level of savings it so sorely needed. The fragmentation data indicated that without larger-scale organizational changes, neither tradi-

Figure 3-5: Sample Process Fragmentation Table

Process:	Indivs.[a]	FTE[b]	Frag. Ratio[c]	Avg. %[d]
PRIORITY Recruit/retain faculty	94	19.2	4.9	20
Generate external funds	89	17.1	5.2	19
Establish infrastructure	24	3.4	7.1	14
Manage project finances	102	25.5	4.0	25
Hire/retain post doc. candidates	43	11.6	3.7	26
BACKGROUND Close project finances	31	3.0	10.4	10
Hire/retain staff	74	19.5	3.8	25
Procure goods	291	41.0	7.1	14
Manage facilities	155	23.0	6.8	15
Manage access to information	79	37.6	2.1	48

[a] Number of individual staff members who indicated they had participated in the process.

[b] The number of individual staff involved expressed as full-time equivalents (FTE), based on the percentage of time spent by each individual on the process.

[c] Fragmentation ratio. The ratio of individuals to FTEs, it indicates the degree of fragmentation in the process, i.e. the process is structured such that no person spends most of his or her time on it. The higher the ratio, the more fragmented the process.

[d] Average percent. The ratio of FTEs to individuals multiplied by 100, it indicates the average percentage of time an individual spends on the process.

tional downsizing nor TQM techniques appeared to offer real opportunities for the School of Medicine to achieve and sustain its administrative cost saving.

A New Organizational Construct

Faced with low customer satisfaction, high costs, and high fragmentation data, the School of Medicine explored the implications of business process re-engineering on its staffing, costs, and organization. It was fortuitous that Stanford University was already engaged in several campuswide process re-engineering initiatives: the process by which staff and faculty "buy/pay" for goods and services and the methods by which proposals for research funding are generated and submitted. Each of the university re-engineering teams had produced a conceptual model identifying a radical new process by which to procure and pay for goods and to develop and submit research proposals. Using the university's conceptual redesigns, the school began an exercise designed to identify the ways in which these new campuswide processes could enable it to restructure its administration. Concurrent with receipt of the university's redesigned processes, a front-end financial software package would become available which would allow the school to change significantly the way in which departments manage financial transactions. The financial management system would eliminate the need for shadow systems and time-consuming reconciliation processes. Subsequently, it would enable departments to eliminate positions that exist solely to maintain the shadow systems.

The result of the school's effort to model the effect of the proposed Stanford University redesigns on the school's organization resulted in the conceptualization of an administrative organizational model that would:

1. Uncouple the administrative organization from the academic organization.
2. Organize administrative units around priority processes focused on the support of individual faculty.
3. Organize administrative units around background processes focused on maintaining reliable and responsive institutional systems that deliver minimally invasive services and support to the priority processes.
4. Staff administrative units with fewer people more focused on specific process area and operating with much greater authority to support the desired products and outputs.

At the heart of this model is the creation of several process teams to support the school's identity processes. For example, the school envisions a team of talented staff who would act as research process managers (RPMs) and support the end-to-end pre- and post-award process. These process managers would have delegated signature authority and be empowered to bust away bureaucracy, although they would report to a process owner, the associate dean for research, and would be accountable to their customer (the faculty) for getting proposals out in a timely manner and for providing support to principal investigators (PIs) in the management of their research funds. Technology would be a key enabler for the process. In addition to providing templates for proposals, new software solutions would help process managers oversee the day-to-day financial operations of the project. Research process managers would not have academic departmental reporting relationships. They may serve faculty from a number of departments. Decoupling research administration support from the narrow boundaries of the academic department would enable the school to reduce the number of staff members participating in the process by 50 percent. The school envisions involving other process managers in the student recruitment and retention process as well as in the faculty recruitment and retention process.

The high-level conceptual design of the new organization is presented in figure 3-6. The success of the School of Medicine's model depends on Stanford University's continuing campuswide re-engineering efforts. The maintenance of large numbers of staff to participate in "broken" university background processes is an expense that the school ca no longer afford. The new high-level buy/pay process intends to deliver processes so simple and straightforward that every member of the Stanford community will become "a shopper" and will be able to procure more goods without the help of process navigators or procurement specialists.

The efforts of the school's team to untangle administrative cost from its academic departments provide lessons for other institutions contemplating re-engineering. To date most re-engineering efforts stop at the door of a school or academic department; little work has been undertaken to realize the results promised by re-engineering. The school's hard look at the structure and organization of the administrative tasks within an academic department indicates that substantial change is possible. In general radical change is possible in higher education if institutions are bold in their approach to redesign and do not set limits or boundaries on the process.

Figure 3-6: Proposed Administrative Organization Chart — Stanford University School of Medicine

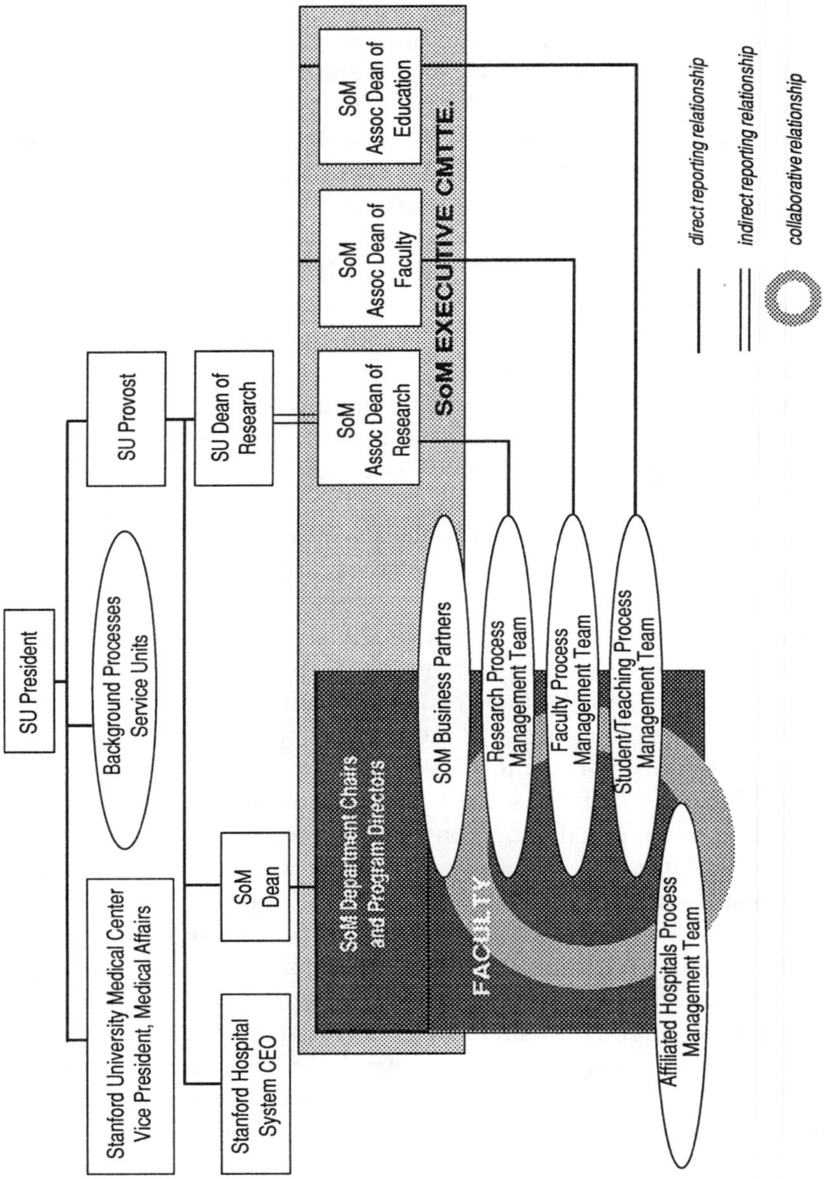

Conclusion

Is it actually possible for higher education to achieve the results promised by re-engineering? Does corporate restructuring have any relevance for academia? Is a radically different organization model possible?

The answers to these questions are: Yes. Yes. And, yes. Radical change is possible. This transformation will not be an easy task, nor will it happen overnight. In fact, the road to a transformed institution can be treacherous. It requires both stamina and a dedication to goals that may at times seem impossible to attain in higher education. The road to transformation begins by requiring that college and university administrators establish a healthy skepticism regarding the status quo and be ready to let go of traditional approaches. An essential ingredient for success will be the desire, inclination, and ability of people from disparate functions across the institution to work together cohesively to develop a new business model.

Therein is the most difficult challenge. *Designing* the new model is easy. *Achieving consensus* around a new business model, however, is fraught with difficulty. Most colleges and universities are characterized by a highly decentralized, boundary-sensitive environment in which responsibility centers usually focus on maximizing their own benefits rather than taking a "What's best for the institution?" view. In most institutions, there is an apparent lack of a "tiebreaking" structure to make tough decisions. Unlike the corporate sector, in which top-down decisions to change are made more readily, higher education's current business model does not provide an efficient decision-making mechanism for change.

However, restructuring will cause an institution's leadership to wrestle with important issues regarding the role and responsibilities of its campuswide, university-provided functions, school-based central administrative functions, and departmentally based administrative functions. In short, by re-engineering, an institution's leadership will be answering the fundamental underlying question: What is the most appropriate business model for a complex, decentralized organization?

The answer will ultimately be one of organizational design: To what extent is the institution willing to "go horizontal," moving from a functionally oriented organization (vertical) to a "process" organization? How much will employees be empowered to operate in teams and make decisions about their processes without going through the organizational hierarchy? These can be difficult questions. Failure to address them consciously throughout the organizational change process may thwart the success of any attempt to change. However, confronting these questions directly and aggressively can enable an institution to re-engineer itself successfully, saving substantial costs and positioning itself strategically for the future.

Notes

1. Michael Hammer and James Champy, *Re-engineering the Corporation: A Manifesto for Business Revolution* (New York: HarperCollins, 1993), p.11.
2. D. Quinn Mills, *Rebirth of the Corporation* (New York: Wiley, 1991), pp. 13–14.
3. Gifford Pinchot and Elizabeth Pinchot, *The End of Bureaucracy and the Rise of the Intelligent Organization* (San Francisco: Berrett-Koehler Publishers, 1993), p. 5.
4. These terms were coined by Ellen M. Knapp of Coopers & Lybrand L.L.P.
5. "Special Report: Rethinking Work," *Business Week*, October 17, 1994, p. 85.
6. Hammer and Champy, *Re-engineering the Corporation*, p. 121.

Meeting the Challenges of Change at Kent State

4

Myron S. Henry

This chapter is based on two presentations delivered by the author early in the 1995 fiscal year. In the first of these, "Meeting the Challenges of Restructuring: Resources, Roles, and Rewards," the author was a member of a two-person panel charged with sharing experiences and insights into the process of restructuring the academic program to promote efficiency and improve quality. The second presentation, "The Need for a More Encompassing View of Scholarship," was delivered in collaboration with Kent State University colleague Greer Glazer. Although the ideas presented in this chapter come from restructuring and reallocation processes implemented at Kent State University, they are applicable to any institution that plans to undergo similar changes.

In most states and at many colleges and universities, meeting the challenges of restructuring has translated into doing more with less in an effort to stay afloat in a climate of constrained or declining resources. Restructuring and change at Kent State University have been driven not only by fiscal constraints but also by a need to rethink curricula, the roles and responsibilities of faculty and staff, and the operations of major functional units (e.g., departments and schools).

The Situation at Kent State

Kent State is a Carnegie Research II institution with an enrollment of approximately 32,000 students at its eight campuses, including 22,000 at the Kent campus. In the spring of 1992, the economy in Ohio was in a steep nose dive, which meant major reductions in state appropriations to public universities. Reductions to the base budget of the Academic Affairs Division on the Kent campus eventually totaled about $8 million, just less than 8 percent of the general fund budget for the division. Deans and other unit heads were asked to develop fiscal year 1993 budget reduction plans. With few exceptions, these plans offered only short-term solutions, perhaps because of uncertainty surrounding the size of reductions the state would require, hopes that the economy would turn around, and the possibility of revenue enhancement measures being enacted at the state level.

What occurred at Kent State that spring paralleled the November 1993 issue of the Pew Higher Education Roundtable *Policy Perspectives* observation that, "A deep recession has reduced public funding for higher education, creating a need to find alternative sources of revenue and resulting in few discretionary funds for institutions."[1]

Public Perceptions

While hopes abounded that fiscal problems in Ohio would be short-lived, the leadership at Kent State recognized that the challenges for higher education in Ohio and across the country were going to be long-term. Higher education was already facing significant shifts and trends in its working environment, including

- the challenge of serving increasing numbers of less well-prepared students;
- a need for states to commit more dollars to other priorities, such as medical care, prison capacity, and law enforcement expansion;
- court cases requiring states to increase funding for elementary and secondary education;
- declining enrollments at colleges and universities in many areas of the country;
- a new, almost hyper-consumer attitude among students;
- student expectations of direct connections between a degree and employment;
- a growing public belief that students are being awarded baccalaureate degrees without being properly educated;
- technology based competition; and
- a public perception that higher education is out of touch with the realities of the 1990s.

The most disturbing factor for public colleges and universities, however, has been their apparent fall from grace with public policymakers, and the increasingly loud chants for more regulation and micromanagement of public universities by the legislative and executive branches of government. As stated in the April 1994 Pew Higher Education Roundtable *Policy Perspectives: To Dance with Change,* "The real anger at higher education comes principally from the makers and shapers of public policy—governors, legislators, regulators, heads of public agencies, and surprisingly, an increasing number from the world of private philanthropy."[2]

Reconceptualizing Scholarship

By the spring of 1992, many in and out of the academy were raising questions about faculty roles and responsibilities. Perhaps more than any other single publication, Ernest Boyer's book, *Scholarship Reconsidered: Priorities of the Professoriate,*[3] spurred universities, including Kent State, to re-examine the nature of faculty scholarship and the implications a more encompassing notion of scholarship might have on faculty roles and responsibilities and on unit productivity.

Processes and Outcomes
Faculty Senate Commission on Scholarship

With encouragement from President Carol A. Cartwright, the Faculty Senate took the lead at Kent State in scholarship reconsideration when it established the Commission on Scholarship in December of 1991. The commission's main task was to consider whether the approach advocated by Boyer or some modification of it was congruent with the faculty's idea of scholarship; whether it could be used as a framework for merit, promotion, and tenure decisions; and if it might be part of a redesign of program evaluation. The commission's work resulted in a report called "Principles for the Evaluation and Reward of Faculty Scholarship" (the Twenty Principles of Scholarship), which presented a plan for reconceptualizing scholarship around the Boyer ideas of the scholarships of discovery, teaching, application, and integration. The report also included operational statements that encouraged departments and schools to review and revise their procedures to ensure that the more encompassing interpretations of scholarship are properly recognized, fostered, rigorously evaluated, and rewarded.

UPBAC

To help faculty and staff at the university become more aware of national and state issues in higher education and to provide advice on university priorities in the face of budget constraints, President Cartwright formed the 27-person, widely representative University Priorities and Budget Advisory Committee (UPBAC) in the fall of 1991. This committee, which is chaired by the provost, was expected to play a major role in priority setting and restructuring, and in communicating with colleagues about the issues affecting higher education.

After much discussion on short and long-term issues at national and state levels that were likely to affect Kent State, the committee developed the Kent Institutional Characteristics (KICS) statement. The KICS statement interprets and expands upon Kent State's mission statement in 11 categories: students, faculty, curriculum, special features, teaching, research and creativity, outreach and community service, campus environment and co-curricular activities, diversity, alumni, and evaluation. The KICS statement, which was intended to offer a shortened, coherent view of a large, complex university, was endorsed by the Faculty Senate and approved by the Board of Trustees during the 1993 spring semester.

Pew Roundtables

Toward the end of the 1992–93 academic year, Kent State was selected as one of the first 30 institutions to participate in a Pew Charitable Trusts sponsored Higher Education Roundtable. The Kent Pew Roundtables brought 25 university opinion leaders together for an evening of discussion on issues and a one-day workshop. Held in the late spring and mid-summer of 1993, these discussions were open, spirited, and constructive. Participants used the roundtable as a basis for a Kent Pew Roundtable position paper, which was ultimately circulated widely and discussed in a variety of open forums. Two of the position paper's five major points are highlighted below.[4]

1. Cultivate a stakeholder-oriented strategy for the university with:
    (a) shared decision making and shared accountability,
    (b) a vital spirit of community, and
    (c) teamwork, unit productivity, and group rewards (in addition to individual rewards).

2. Plan and set priorities according to focus, shared beliefs, values, and the KICS categories.

Strategic Plan

The KICS statement and the Kent Pew Roundtable position paper set the stage for an even more ambitious effort, the development of a universitywide strategic plan. This process proved more challenging than expected, primarily because of ongoing budget constraints and a mandate from the Ohio Board of Regents to all public colleges and universities in Ohio to prepare "Functional Mission Statements" (strategic plans) over a summer and fall semester. At an institution with a long tradition of faculty participation in governance (including collective bargaining), the early challenges centered on persuading departments, schools, and colleges that a strategic plan could be completed in the time allotted, and that unit strategic plans, which were to be developed mostly in the summer of 1993, would be fundamental to the universitywide plan.

To preserve continuity, the 43-member Committee for University Strategic Planning (CUSP) was built around the already cohesive 27-member UPBAC. Other members of CUSP, which was chaired by the provost, were chosen because of their proven reputations as statespeople and leaders. Considerable time was devoted within CUSP and among academic units to promoting a guiding principle for strategic planning: "Think of the university as a whole and how your unit can and does connect to others."

In late January of 1994, after much campus input, revision, and promoting, part one of the Kent State University Strategic Plan, "Academic and Student Affairs," was endorsed by the Faculty Senate and approved by the Board of Trustees. Part two of the strategic plan, "Support Services," was completed and approved in June of 1994.

Summer 1994 Budget Reduction

In contrast to the short-term approaches employed in the $8 million reduction in academic affairs for fiscal year 1993, a second, $3 million reduction for fiscal year 1995 was steered by the following strategic planning objectives:

1. Buffer areas of enrollment growth

2. Buffer units substantially involved in maintaining Carnegie Research II status
3. Minimize impact on selected distinctive programs in accord with the strategic plan
4. Allow for some reallocation to selected strategic plan initiatives (e.g., the new undergraduate studies unit)
5. Minimize reductions in graduate student support
6. Minimize reductions in current expense funding
7. Use selective attrition to reduce faculty and staff positions
8. If revenue exceeds expectations, focus restorations on current expenses, selected faculty positions, and graduate student support

Top 10 Areas of Change at Kent State

This section presents some examples of restructuring and change that resulted from the strategic planning process, the Kent Pew Roundtables, and the work of UPBAC and other Kent State committees. This list is grounded in Kent State experiences, but based on national publications, featured topics at national forums, and discussions with colleagues at other colleges and universities, it is a safe bet that these issues appear on other campuses' top 10 lists as well.

1. Consolidate and eliminate programs and units. Kent State's strategic plan urges more program focus within department, schools, colleges, and divisions. And restructuring for more focus is occurring. Within the College of Business Administration, 10 options in the Ph.D. program have been reduced to six, and three undergraduate majors have been discontinued. The School of Theatre, which discontinued its Ph.D. program in 1994, merged with the Dance Program to become the School of Theatre and Dance. The School of Library and Information Sciences has been integrated into the communication cluster within the College of Fine and Professional Arts and no longer reports directly to the provost. The Graduate College and the Office of Research and Sponsored Programs have been consolidated into the Division of Research and Graduate Studies, saving over $250,000 in administrative costs. The Provost's Office eliminated one associate provost's position, and five of seven regional campuses discontinued assistant deans' positions.

2. Reduce undue program complexity. Overly complex curricula make advising more complicated and may increase the time it takes to complete baccalaureate degrees, something less affluent students can ill afford. At Kent State, some requirements of majors intrude into universal liberal education requirements, and major requirements are frequently too technical and complex. The Kent State Strategic Plan mandates the reduction of undue program complexity to improve retention and graduation rates and free up scarce resources to redirect to new program development. Departments and schools have been asked to find ways of improving learning while reducing credit requirements in the majors. Thus far, progress has been only modest.

3. Improve academic student services. To improve retention, Kent State's strategic plan emphasized the importance of establishing an undergraduate studies unit. This unit reports to a new vice provost for undergraduate studies, and is responsible for advising and counseling undergraduate students. A new advising center has been established in a central location, and most administrative offices in undergraduate studies have been located in a facility adjacent to the advising center. All services of undergraduate studies unit, including advising students with undeclared majors, will be fully functional by the spring of 1996.

4. Increase support and recognition of teaching. To further support instructional development and recognize teaching, a University Teaching Council has been established at Kent State. The council is responsible for allocating up to $100,000 annually to support the improvement of teaching, with a particular attention to the undergraduate level and the use of new technologies. In the fall of 1995, the council sponsored a highly successful second annual two-day conference, Celebrating Excellence in College Teaching 95, which focused in part on the use of new technologies in student learning.

Kent State is also one of a dozen universities participating in an American Association for Higher Education (AAHE) national pilot project, From Idea to Prototype: A Peer Review of Teaching.[5] Participating units include the Department of History, the School of Nursing, and the Department of Mathematics and Computer Science. A goal of this project is to develop additional rigorous and documentable ways of evaluating the scholarship of teaching.

5. Revisit faculty roles. Legislatures and executive branches of government have taken a keen interest in the amount of time faculty devote to undergraduate instructional activities. National surveys show that faculty believe too much emphasis is placed on research and that other activities like teaching are not rewarded to the extent that research is.

The AAHE Forum on Faculty Roles and Rewards and the national Pew Roundtables as well as other national conversations have given new energy to the topic of how faculty spend their professional time and how they are (or should be) compensated. Kent State is also giving attention to this, as the following three principles from the Twenty Principles of Scholarship illustrate:

- All four aspects of scholarship need to be considered and rewarded at the department and school levels.
- Criteria should respond fully to the diverse aspects of faculty roles.
- Weighting of criteria may differ for faculty with differential roles and rank.

6. Encourage and serve diversity on campus. Kent State continues to implement plans to increase diversity as mandated by strategic plan goals and an earlier diversity report. Of Kent State's 47 deans, chairs, and directors, 17 are women or from underrepresented groups; eight of these 17 have been appointed in the last two years. In collaboration with the leadership of the Faculty Senate, a Subcommittee on Diversity in the Curriculum has been charged, among other things, to work with the Liberal Education Requirements (LER) Curriculum Committee to find ways to encourage departments and schools to revise existing LER courses to assure that diversity elements are pervasive throughout the liberal education program whenever appropriate.

7. Promote community on campus. In its strategic plan and through the Kent Pew Roundtables, Kent State has stressed the need for a "vital spirit of community." This has meant promoting constructive dialogue among students, faculty, and staff; fostering respect for differing points of view; stressing common courtesy; and providing forums for reasoned conversation on complex social issues. In the fall of 1994, the university sponsored a forum featuring an evening with Amitai Etzioni, author of *The Spirit of Community*, and organized a Kent Pew Roundtable panel discussion on decision making and accountability.

8. Improve communication on campus. As complex institutions, colleges and universities experience their share of communication snags. Some recent examples of successful communication at Kent State include the development of the 1994 North Central Association reaccreditation self-study and the strategic plan; the Kent Pew Roundtables, periodic reports by the president and provost at Faculty Senate meetings, regular town-meeting-type visits by the provost to departments and schools, and receptions for faculty and staff hosted by the Board of Trustees and by the president. Each college, school, and department has been asked to go the extra mile to ensure that colleagues are informed about major issues, and each individual is asked to make an effort to stay informed. All colleagues are asked to be tolerant in cases where communication should have been better.

9. Embrace new technologies and distance learning. In recognition of the major role new technologies will play inside and outside of the academy, two reports on computing, the *Network and Information Systems Study* and the *Academic Computing Study* have been completed at Kent State during the last two years. Many of the recommendations from the first report are being or have been implemented, such as the installation of a new mainframe, a fiber-optic backbone, and cable and wiring in the residence halls. Another task force has been at work developing plans to convert historic Moulton Hall into an instructional technologies and distributive learning center. The task force is also responsible for the development of a pilot electronic classroom to be located in the library. Electronic linkages will play a key role in making instruction more accessible to students at all eight Kent State University campuses. Already, several regional campuses are involved in interactive video linkages with public schools in their respective regions. IBM representatives are partners with the university in the development of the Moulton Hall and pilot electronic classroom projects, and plans are being developed to raise private money for these projects.

10. Engage in regional collaboration. Fostering regional collaboration is a major goal from the Kent State University Strategic Plan. Provosts from the University of Akron, Cleveland State University, Kent State, Youngstown State University (40 miles east of Kent), and the Northeast Ohio Universities College of Medicine (eight miles east of Kent) meet on a regular basis to discuss issues of mutual interest and promote a consortial point of view instead of institution-specific ones. Achieving new levels of collaboration among northeast Ohio institutions will depend on presidential leadership, changes in institutional incentive structures and behaviors, cooperative and innovative uses of new technologies, commitment to the regional good by local politicians as well as institutions, and recognition by the involved institutions that bigger is neither better nor more affordable.

Conclusion

As exemplified through Boyer's idea of the scholarships of teaching, integration, application, and discovery, a continuum of equally important scholarly activities that are complementary, mutually supportive, and unifying is essential to a successful academic program. Departmental productivity should be judged over an array of equally important tasks embodied within the overall mission of the unit. This approach does mean, in the words of Eugene Rice of AAHE, "thinking more in terms of our work instead of mostly about my work." It means highlighting unit productivity in the context of the mission of the university. And it means valuing university citizenship as well as professional associations.

How do universities promote strategies that will facilitate a greater sense of community and collective success among major operational units? How should institutions evaluate and reward unit productivity as well as individual achievement? How do those in the academy learn to stop overemphasizing the importance of research and recognize that the validity of all forms of scholarship depend on more extensive and rigorous evaluation? What are the responsibilities of faculty, administration, and staff to foster needed changes and restructuring in times of resource constraints? The complex issues that emanate from these questions are at the heart of successful restructuring and change. Addressing these will demand leadership from the faculty, administration, and staff of higher education institutions.

Notes

1. Robert Zemsky, ed., "An Uncertain Terrain," *Policy Perspectives,* Nov. 1993, vol. 5, no. 2, section A (Philadelphia, Pa.: Pew Higher Education Roundtable), p. 2A.

2. Robert Zemsky, ed., "To Dance with Change," *Policy Perspectives*, April 1994, vol. 5, no. 3, section A (Philadelphia, Pa.: Pew Higher Education Roundtable), p. 6A.

3. Ernest L. Boyer, *Scholarship Reconsidered: Priorities of the Professoriate* (Princeton, N.J.: The Carnegie Foundation for the Advancement of Teaching, 1990).

4. Greer Glazer and M.S. Henry, "Approaches to Conducting Workload Studies: A Case Study at Kent State University," in *New Directions for Institutional Research: Analyzing Faculty Workload*, J.F. Wergin, ed. (San Francisco, Calif.: Jossey-Bass, 1994), p. 39.

5. Myron S. Henry, "Almost Metropolitan Universities," *Metropolitan Universities*, vol. 5, no. 3 (1994): 41.

New Paradigms in Student Affairs   5

Paula M. Rooney
P. Gerard Shaw

On college and university campuses across the country, the role of student affairs is constantly changing. Once recognized as a profession within higher education and a field of study in academe, student affairs has transformed itself many times over during this century. This transformation continues today as administrators explore new reporting structures for their institutions in response to changing economic climate and customer demand. The purpose of this chapter is to provide a background on the history of student affairs, describe the changes many institutions are currently undergoing in the area of student affairs, and offer a preview of the student affairs paradigm of the future.

A Brief History of Student Affairs

In the early days of American higher education, faculty were the traditional providers of student services on college and university campuses. College instructors felt a responsibility toward the intellectual, religious, and moral development of their students, and this responsibility extended beyond the classroom into student life. In addition to their teaching duties, faculty lived in residences with students, coached athletic teams, provided career counseling, and handled disciplinary problems.

Under this structure, which was heavily influenced by the British system, each residence hall housed a faculty member or tutor. With students ranging in age from 14 to 20, strict rules were created to maintain order in the residence halls and on campus. Faculty were charged with enforcing these rules.

This relationship between faculty and students changed however as American faculty began pursuing their advanced degrees abroad, particularly in Germany. There they found their European counterparts to be far more interested in research than in the lives of their students outside the classroom. Along with their new degrees, these American faculty members brought back with them to the United States a new indifference toward student life and heightened interest in research.

To cope with their faculty's shift in focus, colleges and universities began appointing individuals to specifically handle student affairs. Such an individual was usually referred to as the dean of men or dean of women. Harvard University was the first to appoint a dean of men, and by the late nineteenth century, many colleges and universities had created such positions. As the twentieth century began, these deans took on more responsibilities involving students' out-of-the-classroom experience. Much of their work was rooted in a holistic approach that focused heavily on the general well-being of the students.

In 1916, Teacher's College, Columbia University, offered the first formal student affairs program. This new field of study continued to expand over the years, and in 1937 the American Council on education published a document titled "The Student Personnel Point of View." This publication, which assessed the student affairs area, marked the official recognition of student affairs as a profession and a field of study.

Since 1937, student affairs has continued to grow, developing administratively to the point where every campus has a chief student affairs officer, and many such officers serve on the president's cabinet or senior staff. Student affairs officers have taken the lead in recognizing and serving students' needs and differences.

The Current Paradigm

Most college and university organizational charts look alike: there is a president, a provost (on some campuses), and a number of vice presidents or deans (e.g., academic affairs, student affairs, financial affairs, and institutional advancement). Each vice president or dean has a number of department chairs reporting to him or her, and this structure promotes accountability and ensures clear lines of responsibility.

The budget process at most institutions is designed to work through this hierarchy. A department determines its needs, the department chair submits the request in a predetermined budget process, the request is approved, modified, or rejected, and the department is held responsible for managing the finally approved budget. Requests flow up the organizational model, responses come down, and ongoing accountability is maintained.

The autonomy that this current model creates has worked well for faculty and administrators, because it allows for flexibility and enables departments to take on new responsibilities. Under this model, new courses are developed, new programs are initiated, and new services are provided by whichever department recognizes the need and is able to provide the service. Usually, this need is met by one department, and very little is shared between departments. Specialties have developed within this autonomy, and student affairs has seen its own specializations grow over the past few decades. The field that began with deans of men and women has expanded to include career counseling, residential life, athletics, and activities.

The needs of students, faculty, and administrators are changing rapidly, however, and the old solution of creating new programs to meet their needs is no longer feasible in these tighter economic times.

The autonomy that departments within colleges and universities once enjoyed is now becoming a roadblock to providing cost-effective and efficient services.

In the student affairs area, the need for a new paradigm is clearly illustrated in the changing relationship between the student affairs and academic affairs departments on many campuses. Recent studies show that faculty are migrating toward concentrations in their fields of study and away from loyalty to an institution or even a department. In the process of changing, faculty have given up many of their traditional roles, and—because new programs are not being created—student affairs professionals have taken up the slack. Today, many student affairs areas include such responsibilities as academic advising in addition to the more traditional areas of residence life and career counseling.

The New Paradigm

Students at colleges and universities are more aware of their role as customers, and their expectations of educational institutions are higher than ever before. Along with their parents, students are looking for greater returns on investments. (For example, admissions directors are getting more questions about placement rates for jobs and graduate programs.) But some would argue that while students are asking for more from higher education, they are arriving on campus with less to offer. Today's students are not as well prepared academically by national standards. In addition, more students with diagnosed learning disabilities are entering the higher education system, and many institutions are unequipped to provide such students with the necessary support services.

To combat these challenges, administrators are now talking about bringing the in-class and out-of-the-classroom experiences closer together. Some institutions have already restructured in ways that link academic and student affairs organizationally. Some have restructured only in processes that serve students. An example of this type of restructuring is the first year experience program, which is designed to prepare freshmen for the challenges and responsibilities of campus life. Others have not yet implemented changes, but are studying ways to do this in the near future.

The student affairs paradigm has shifted from faculty providing all the services, to specifically trained student affairs professionals providing the service, to a kind of middle ground where faculty and student affairs personnel work together to provide a more holistic educational experience.

On the administrative side, many institutions are restructuring by placing student affairs under the academic area and thus taking away student affairs' direct reporting line to the president. An ongoing dialogue on the Internet dealing with the reporting structure for student affairs reveals that new structures are being implemented on many campuses.

Student affairs personnel are recognizing the need to redefine student affairs. They are discussing how student affairs affects the institution, its relationship with the academic area, and its place in the administration of the institution. Many student affairs professionals are recognizing that they have been reactive, rather than proactive, on campus. For example, because of a failure to recognize and plan ahead for such issues as diversity, some student affairs professionals have had to react to crisis situations on their campuses. This approach has had positive and negative impacts. Positively, they are sensitive to and aware of students' needs and this knowledge is a great asset to the other members of the campus community. Even in a reactive mode, student affairs professionals are the first deal with many student-related issues, and their knowledge of students is a great asset to other members of the campus community. Negatively, a lack of data about the students has hindered their desire to be proactive in recognizing students' needs. One solution to this problem is to collect more data about the students when they enter the institution in their first year.

Due to the economics of the future in higher education, the new paradigm for student affairs will not include doing business as usual. There will be less activity with fewer people to accomplish the tasks. Technology will play a major role in servicing student needs. More services provided in the past through regular student fees will be provided on a fee-for-service basis.

In the near future, the manner in which other services traditionally provided by student affairs are delivered will change drastically. Institutions are welcoming a generation of students who are accustomed to receiving service when and where they want it. This "ATM mentality" has changed the demands placed on all service providers in higher education, and student affairs is not immune.

The impact of all this will be to return the student affairs of 60 years ago, with the work being performed by a student affairs generalist. Institutions can no longer afford specialists. First year experience programs are pioneering the return of this generalist who can educate students outside the classroom as well as function administratively. More and more frequently, students seeking help with a problem involving registration, academic advising, or other areas are getting the information they need from a well-trained student affairs professional who knows the students and the institution.

Co-curricular activities complementing classroom activity are growing, and the relationship between student affairs and academic affairs is deepening. Student affairs professionals are being recognized on campus as co-educators. Their insight is sought by faculty looking for more information about the students they see in their classrooms. Student affairs programs are being designed to complement the classroom experience, and more and more students are taking advantage of the service opportunities provided.

At Dean College, the traditional dean of students position has been replaced with a dean for campus life and a dean for advising and academic support. The dean for campus life is responsible for residence life, student activities, the health center, counseling center, first year experience program, and judicial affairs. The dean for advising and academic support is responsible for academic advising, academic support services, academic monitoring of student progress, transfer advising, articulation agreements with other institutions, and career counseling. These deans report to the vice president/dean of the college, who is the senior academic officer.

This restructuring was done with the objective of creating a total learning environment. Under the leadership of one academic officer, all departments are united in contributing to the total education of the students. There was little resistance to the change and personnel have been working together to provide a more comprehensive educational experience. How this will work itself out in the future remains to be seen. Like all change, it will have to be continually evaluated and modified where necessary.

The new paradigm is evolving at other campuses, as well. Student affairs and academic affairs are uniting in new and unique organizational structures as a result of this new emphasis on creating a more complete learning environment.

Conclusion

The emergence of closer working ties between student affairs and academic affairs signals an increased emphasis on the primary purpose of higher education institutions: to educate students.

Because the student affairs paradigm shift is still evolving, its ultimate effect on colleges at universities remains to be seen. The return to the student affairs generalist will change student affairs at many colleges and universities and may produce cost savings. Since these professionals will be able to operate cross functionally, the specialists will no longer exist on the campus. More efficient operations and more effective education will also result. It will, and in some instances already has, produce better customer service for students and faculty. Colleges and universities of the future will be well served as a result.

Organizational Restructuring at Carnegie Mellon University

6

Patrick J. Keating
Neal F. Binstock
John A. Fry
Philip J. Goldstein
Alfonso de Lucio

For many colleges and universities, the need to survive in an increasingly competitive marketplace is the driving force behind organizational change. Factors such as declining revenues and growing pressure on expenditures for financial aid, benefits, and salaries are forcing institutions to consider new approaches to fulfilling their missions. The purpose of this chapter is to illustrate how one institution, Carnegie Mellon University, created and implemented a strategy for process restructuring and present a model for other institutions facing similar needs for organizational change.

The Push for Change

At Carnegie Mellon University, the factors driving the need for organizational change include the desire to fulfill the institution's vision, general economic forces that are affecting all higher education institutions, a set of conditions and forces specific to Carnegie Mellon, and a growing need to provide a higher level and quality of service.

Carnegie Mellon's vision is to be a leading educational institution that is innovative in its approach to education, research, and service. The institution's desire for leadership and innovation forces it to be proactive and change-oriented. The traditional strengths of the institution, supported by comparative advantages in its application of technology, positions it well for the future.

Carnegie Mellon faces several pressures that constrain its financial position and demand new thinking about how to achieve its vision and mission. The current research environment is highly competitive and somewhat unfriendly. Funding for research experi-

mentation and support for costs related to administration and facility operations are being questioned in Washington, D.C. In addition,
tuition costs at Carnegie Mellon have risen to the point that future
increases will be limited to the rate of inflation. Financial aid as an
expenditure has been growing rapidly, reducing the marginal rate of
return of tuition increases. The institution's endowment, while highly
diversified and well invested, is not competitive with peer institutions
on a per faculty or per student basis. At the same time, the market for
fund raising on which Carnegie Mellon will be relying is becoming
increasingly competitive.

The institution's support service functions are generally lean and
under constant pressure to improve services and lower costs. This
pressure will only increase as the financial environment tightens further. The desire to improve services spans well beyond the administrative area of the institution to services that are provided to students,
including undergraduate education, student life, and social and rec-
reational activities.

Carnegie Mellon operates in a highly competitive market for students, faculty, research funding, and donations. The culture of the
institution is entrepreneurial, strategic in its approach, and market-
niche oriented. As a result, a high degree of sensitivity to the need
for change exists across the campus. These factors, combined with
the character of the institution, make change at Carnegie Mellon a
constant rather than an exception.

The call for change at Carnegie Mellon comes from a variety of
individuals and groups. The board of trustees is proactive with and
supportive of the institution's vision, and encourages the move to
improve services and lower costs. The president and the executive
group, including deans, are working to develop initiatives and programs that will produce organizational change. Within the administrative support areas of the university, change is being driven at the
senior management level in response to the need to lower costs and
improve services. At all levels of the organization, faculty and staff
are beginning to understand that Carnegie Mellon must change to
achieve future improvement.

Organization for the Next Century

The forces driving change at Carnegie Mellon offer clues as to
how the institution might organize itself in the future. On the aca-

demic side, Carnegie Mellon is a strong, interdisciplinary organization with significant cross-department and cross-disciplinary activities, both in research and education. Such activities will likely grow in the future, especially given the institution's vision for innovation in programs and services. Further, technology is expected to facilitate the blurring of the boundaries between disciplines and programs.

The academic departments are dealing with advances in technology that will allow programs to be delivered in very different ways. Internet, CD-ROM, multi-media, powerful and inexpensive desktop and laptop computers, and high speed networks will likely produce significant opportunities for introducing new educational delivery systems. Although some have predicted that this new technology will replace traditional classroom learning with distance learning, this scenario is unlikely at Carnegie Mellon and other institutions where education entails broad interaction with colleagues and mentors in academic, social, and cultural learning.

For administrative units, significant changes lie ahead for Carnegie Mellon and other higher education institutions. The administrative component will become smaller in response to major economic forces requiring colleges and universities to be more efficient, effective, and able to deliver better service at lower costs. The traditional set of administrative or support service departments will soon become obsolete or disappear. People and technologies will be organized around a particular service or work process rather than a single function, such as accounting, payroll, or student registration. Organizations will be more likely to form around work processes such as financial management information services, sponsored-research support services, student enrollment services, and the acquisition of goods and services. While such work processes are evolving, the organizations themselves will have to evolve and change.

The skills required to provide these services in the future will also change significantly. Staff will be trained in analytical thinking, project management, use of technologies, communications, and leadership. Multi-purpose, multi-skilled individuals will replace specialists trained to fulfill a single purpose; staff members will be fewer in number but more highly paid.

Teamwork, as it is evolving today, will become a more significant part of the future organization of Carnegie Mellon University and other institutions. Services and problems will be addressed with a multifaceted set of skills and tools by teams with significant authority and power. These teams will be able to identify and solve problems and put in place policies and procedures that will deliver better service. This will eliminate hierarchy and distribute power and authority to staff who are closer to the end customer (e.g., students, faculty, and alumni).

Reliance on the use of outside expertise (outsourcing) to provide administrative services will increase. The test of the market, which administrative services will increasingly be subject to, will result in more outsourcing. Such a move will allow for significant efficiencies and take advantage of economies of scale in delivery of services. In today's resource-constrained environment, it no longer makes sense for a university to invest in the expertise required to operate a diverse set of businesses. For specialized services, universities will seek partnerships with private corporations as long as quality standards are being maintained.

Achieving the Vision

Major organizational changes require a broad set of approaches. The tools and approaches being developed and implemented at Carnegie Mellon include visioning, total quality management (TQM), benchmarking, interactive skills, meeting management techniques, and the use of teams charged with continuous improvement, problem solving, or radical re-engineering objectives. At Carnegie Mellon, these quality tools are being put to use most extensively to improve services and reduce costs in the administrative area.

A quality improvement team was used to oversee the process for designing and constructing building renovations across the campus. Other quality teams are involved in the areas of registration, financial aid, communications between physical plant and its customer departments, and gift tracking. In several key areas, the institution has taken the more radical approach of re-engineering. The acquisitions process (i.e., acquiring of goods and services on campus) has undergone re-engineering, and three other major service areas are being studied for potential re-engineering: sponsored research, enrollment administration, and the financial management process. Carnegie Mellon's acquisitions re-engineering process is described in greater detail in the next section.

Carnegie Mellon is providing employee training in TQM tools, interactive skill behaviors, and now re-engineering. In addition, promotion has begun for training in areas such as leadership skills for management, project management skills for project leaders, and analytical and technical skills for staff. These training initiatives ensure Carnegie Mellon's ability to effectively analyze its services and develop new approaches to providing them.

To support these improvement initiatives, Carnegie Mellon is developing new compensation programs and reward and recognition systems. Currently, employees spend a significant amount of their time working together on a project to solve a problem or improve a service. Because they rarely work alone on a particular task, individual contributions are often overshadowed by team contributions. The new compensation systems will be designed to reflect such activities and include concepts such as bonus payments, gain sharing, or special incentives.

Further, rewards and recognition for effort need to be more prevalent within the institution. Carnegie Mellon has set up a series of committees to develop criteria and programs for recognizing excellent service and creative contributions. Though efforts are just beginning, these programs promise to have significant positive effects on employees' motivation, interest, and involvement in establishing the future directions of the services they provide.

The Acquisitions Project

Carnegie Mellon's most visible and far-reaching attempt at restructuring its administration is the re-engineering of its procurement-disbursement, or acquisitions, process. Like past improvement initiatives at the university, the acquisitions project was driven by the twin goals of enhanced service and reduced cost. However, unlike other improvement projects that focused on incremental change, this effort sought to rapidly achieve substantial (tenfold) improvements in all measures of the time, cost, and quality of the purchasing process.

As is the case at most universities, customers did not perceive Carnegie Mellon's purchasing department as a good service provider. Historically, the purchasing department focused on processing and monitoring large volumes of paper-based transactions. The department's employees, for the most part, had neither the training nor the mandate to negotiate advantageous purchase agreements or provide attentive service to the university's faculty and staff. As a

result, Carnegie Mellon was paying too much for the goods it ac-
quired, and its faculty and staff had grown increasingly frustrated
with the time and effort required to navigate a purchase through the
university.

Recognizing the potentially large benefits to be gained, Carnegie
Mellon chose the acquisition process as its first attempt at re-engineering. The acquisitions project team (APT), a cross-functional
group of university staff, was formed and charged with—

- reducing the time and effort required to process an order,
- identifying ways to reduce the university's total expenditures for
  goods and services by better leveraging its buying power, and
- reducing the cost of processing purchase orders and invoices by
  eliminating unnecessary activity and using technology.

The development of the APT has been a two-part process. In
December 1993, a small core team was formed to develop a vision for
a new process. The team decided to discard old concepts, start with a
clean slate, and dramatically shift paradigms. No past practice, rule,
or procedure was deemed untouchable, except for the goal of maximizing end customer satisfaction. This change was accomplished
through several days of 'visioning' on what shape the new process
could take. The team was also charged with developing a rationale
for why Carnegie Mellon needed to re-engineer the acquisition process and estimating the benefits it could hope to realize as a result of
the effort. This task was accomplished by analyzing the existing purchasing process and assessing the satisfaction of Carnegie Mellon
employees who were the users of this process. The detailed project
activities performed by the APT are listed below:

- Identify customers
- Identify outputs
- Use process map and flow charts to analyze all current processes
  and systems
- Collect customer requirements
- Benchmark best practices
- Develop metrics (e.g., process cost, and cycle time)
- Identify technology opportunities and solutions
- Assess the value provided by each step in the current process to
  the end customer

This analysis confirmed the university's suspicion regarding the degree to which its acquisition process was "broken." Some of the APT's most revealing findings included the following:

- Carnegie Mellon was spending approximately $48 to process the paperwork associated with each of its 40,000 orders per year.
- It took an average of 64 days from the time a customer decided to make a purchase until that order was received and invoiced.
- Recordkeeping and paper processing took 75 percent of the time spent by the purchasing department to process an order, leaving only 25 percent for negotiation or customer service.
- A minimum of 25 percent of all orders required extensive rework to correct errors that had occurred at an earlier part of the process.

To help develop the new design, customers, stakeholders of the existing process, and administrators were interviewed extensively through focus groups, structured written and face-to-face surveys, and free-form discussions. Customers were very clear about their requirements for any new process. They wanted fast delivery, convenience, the best price, direct contact with the vendor for placing orders and gathering information, direct delivery to the customer, and less paperwork. Customers also wanted central administration to perform or oversee the steps in the new process that added value for the customer, such as contract negotiation and vendor management.

Using the requirements of the customers and the knowledge gained by researching best practices in procurement at other universities and corporations, the team developed a vision for a redesigned acquisitions process. The new design eliminates the need for a paper purchase order through use of a procurement card for the acquisition of all goods and services. The procurement card works like a personal credit card, allowing the cardholder to order goods and services directly from a vendor and offer payment at the time of purchase, eliminating both the paper purchase order and invoice. The second feature of the new process uses "commodity management," working with preferred vendors to reduce the size of the vendor base and realize cost savings on the procurement of goods and services.

A partnership has been developed with a major local bank and a third-party provider of information technology services. Through the third-party provider, significant on-line information will be available relating to acquisitions made by Carnegie Mellon cardholders. This information will enable better identification and tracking of purchases on a much more timely basis than the current system. Moving to preferred vendor agreements through commodity management will provide the university with approximately $8 million in savings. The objective is to reduce the vendor base to less than 1,000 vendors by negotiating competitive price agreements. In addition to cost savings, these vendor contracts will include other terms and conditions to provide a more effective purchasing environment for Carnegie Mellon.

With the completion of the design, the implementation phase of the project began. A new, cross-functional team was created to implement the new process. The team included people from the various functions or organizational areas that would be affected by the new process, as well as people who could provide specific expertise or guidance. The elements of the team are as follows:

- A steering committee to provide general guidance and feedback
- An advisory board consisting of functional area experts to serve as a sounding board for new concepts
- A process owner to provide change management assistance and direct all the resources involved in the process
- A project manager to guide the team and the process
- The Carnegie Mellon Business Managers Council
- Staff involved with public relations, publications, systems and technology, financial services, procurement, human resources, internal audit, clerical and analytical services
- Representatives from Coopers & Lybrand

The primary responsibilities of the implementation team were to complete the detailed process design started by the original APT, choose a bank to provide the procurement card, and develop detailed policies to govern its use. The implementation team was also responsible for devising ways to test the new design and plan for the card's gradual introduction to the university.

To minimize risk and exposure and build the infrastructure necessary to support this new process, pilot testing will occur over a six-month period. During this period, input will be collected from end users, process stakeholders, and departmental coordinators. In addition, a regular inspection of the validity and reliability of the data, as well as the audit trail, will be conducted. The data and the audit trail are expected to be more effective and supportive of purchasing transactions than the current process. Complete campus use of the new process is expected by the spring of 1996. By that time, the conversion away from using purchase orders to using the procurement card will be complete.

The detailed acquisition process that the team eventually developed is very straightforward. Cardholders are assigned a procurement card with a magnetic stripe holding a unique identification number, dollar limits, electronic linkage to responsibility centers, and electronic vendor and commodity type control. To obtain a product or service, the cardholder looks through paper or electronic catalogs and a list of preferred vendors. The order is placed by telephone, electronically or in person; the procurement card number is provided; and the materials are received. Delivery, in most cases, is the end customer's desktop. The bank forwards the details of the just-completed transaction to a database and a third-party provider of information technology services.

Another responsibility of the implementation team is to plan for and execute an employee redeployment program. As a result of the new and more efficient process, 28 positions will be eliminated while nine new positions will be created. Because of the procurement card and direct delivery by preferred vendors, Carnegie Mellon will no longer need an accounts payable department, and the role of receiving and central stores will be drastically reduced. In addition, the job responsibilities of employees of the purchasing department will change dramatically when purchasing's function shifts from processing purchase orders to negotiating preferred vendor agreements, measuring vendor performance, and collecting customer feedback.

Early on in the project, the APT recognized the potential impact that re-engineering would have on some of its employees and it committed itself to assisting their transition to new positions. The team therefore developed an employee transition program with the following basic tenants:

- Affected employees would be notified well before their positions were eliminated.
- All affected employees would be offered another position within the university.
- Carnegie Mellon would support affected employees in their efforts to acquire new skills and increase their potential to acquire new positions.

- Carnegie Mellon would not place anyone in a new job but rather would make employees responsible for taking advantage of the services offered by the university to help them manage their own job search.

As anticipated, employee redeployment proved to be one of the most challenging aspects of the project. It was also one of the most misunderstood, as the team had to address false rumors of large scale layoffs on more than one occasion. These rumors were effectively preempted through the team's communication plan. One of the main priorities of the implementation team has been to keep everyone affected by the change informed about the progress and activities of the project. This goal is being achieved through formal and informal communications. Every affected employee is continuously updated on project developments through a 'buddy' system that is conducive to informal dialogue. The 'buddy' system allows employees to ask questions directly to the implementation team on any issue related to the project. Further, the implementation team developed a timeline that identified when each position would be eliminated or changed. This information was shared with affected employees early on in the implementation phase.

Finally, an employment specialist has been assigned to each affected employee to assist in the transition and facilitate the use of services Carnegie Mellon is offering, including career counseling, special job announcements, resume preparation, practice interviews, skills assessments, and training support.

This new process exceeds the requirements of the end customer at Carnegie Mellon and supports the vision of the organization, providing substantial procurement cost savings, better and easier access to information, reduced cycle time, tasks focused on work processes rather than functional areas, convenience for the end customer, better audit trails, significant internal process cost savings, and performance of many services by organizations outside of Carnegie Mellon so that the university is able to focus on its core businesses of teaching and research.

Long-Term Implications of Organizational Change

The acquisitions project is just the first of many re-engineering efforts planned at Carnegie Mellon. All of these projects will have a significant impact on how the university is organized in terms of its resource allocation, division of responsibilities, and institutional and human resources policies.

Redeployment of staff displaced by these re-engineered processes will continue to be a significant challenge for the institution. The human resources department will need to fundamentally change its focus from regulating, controlling, and inspecting, to providing services to employees that will increase their value to the institution and assist them in redeployment or transition situations.

As these changes take place, responsibility and authority will be delegated lower in the organization and closer to the customer. This means that people who are directly involved with providing services will be empowered to make changes, improve services, and use resources. As such delegation occurs, management will need to change. A manager's span of responsibility may broaden as the organization flattens, but his or her authority and control will decrease. Managers will be expected to delegate responsibility and authority and become more oriented to inspection and coaching oriented than to control. This is one of the most difficult challenges Carnegie Mellon will face, and one that will require specific change management strategies to accomplish. Extensive communication, education, and training is taking place within the management ranks at Carnegie Mellon, and more will be needed.

As Carnegie Mellon continues down the path of process simplification and administrative re-engineering, it is fundamentally altering the relationship between central administration and the schools. Historically, central administration at Carnegie Mellon played two primary roles: processor of administrative transactions and enforcer of university policy. As transaction processing is simplified and more routine aspects are automated, this traditional role of the administration will change. Further, as the institution continues to look for opportunities to privatize aspects of its operations, it will be getting out of some businesses altogether. What emerges then is a new model for central administration that is focused on—

- establishing a management infrastructure that provides the necessary tools (technology, training, etc.) to all staff to enable them to execute their own transactions and manage their own finances, providing only those services in which central administration can be competitive with private corporations,

- establishing and maintaining program performance measures to support management decision-making, and
- becoming an internal advisor and resource to faculty and staff as they compete for research grants, procure goods, manage their finances, and provide services to students.

The changing role of central administration has implications for the way the schools operate as well. Process re-engineering is not focused exclusively on the central administration. Rather, by attempting to improve a process as it cuts across departments, the opportunity to redefine the roles and responsibilities of school-based administration is also created. As processes become more efficient, schools will no longer need to employ as many staff to perform administrative tasks. As new technologies and additional process changes are implemented, deans will be able to dismantle "shadow administrations" and refocus those resources on academic programs and student services.

Even more profoundly, the decentralization of transaction processing and employee empowerment that has so far accompanied Carnegie Mellon's process improvements will require all university employees to share in the responsibility for complying with university policy, adhering to sponsored research regulations, and applying good business judgment to the decisions they make. In today's highly competitive, resource-constrained environment, universities can no longer afford to employ large numbers of administrative staff to review each transaction being executed. This practice is too expensive and hinders responsiveness to customers. Deans, department chairs, faculty, and staff must all share in this responsibility.

Effects of Change on Higher Education

The increasing presence of improvement initiatives like those taking place at Carnegie Mellon are forcing all universities to grapple with several significant changes at the core of how they are administered. University employees can no longer assume that they will stay in the same job, doing the same tasks, year after year. Change is a continuous process, and universities, like corporations, must prepare their employees for a world in which skills need to be updated constantly, jobs change frequently, and entire operations are discontinued if they are unable to provide high quality, cost-effective services.

To help employees prosper in such a demanding world, universities need to disavow the notion that a job is an entitlement. Rather, they must instill in their employees that the key to success in the next century will be to develop the ability to "re-engineer" themselves, so that they are continuously re-tooling their skills to adapt to, and perhaps lead, the changing world around them. To help in this process, universities need to provide a much greater emphasis on job and skills training, establish employee redeployment programs to assist those that are displaced by change, and reward flexibility and creativity.

For these initiatives to succeed, higher education managers must also change. In the new, leaner and more flexible organizations that are emerging, a manager can no longer measure his or her success by the amount of resources controlled. Performance criteria and rewards must be changed so that a manager's rewards are driven by measurable outcomes and results, not headcounts and budgets.

Finally, boards and presidents must play a more active role if administrative change is to be successful. The higher education industry is attempting to make very significant changes that will be resisted by those who feel they are likely to lose out. Large-scale fundamental change cannot be driven by re-engineering teams alone. To be successful, such change must be seen as the top priority of the senior leaders of the institution. Trustees and presidents must educate their campuses about the need for change and provide the vision and leadership needed to help their managers in bringing it about.

It is unlikely that a singular model of organization and administration will emerge in the higher education industry. Each university is different, and the experiences and needs of Carnegie Mellon are not the same as those of Yale University or the University of California. However, the issues and challenges described in this chapter are ones that will be shared by any university that attempts to reap the benefits of administrative restructuring. All universities must reinvent their organizations around a common set of characteristics that includes—

- more flexible and process-oriented structures,
- increased emphasis on and support for the use of teams,
- shared responsibility and accountability between central administration and schools,
- greater investment in the development and training of staff whose skills will need to change many times throughout their lifetime, and

- greater incorporation of suppliers and outsourcing partners as a part of the university administrative structure.

The organization of the future will be characterized by much less rigid distinction between units. Eventually, the lines must be blurred between departments and functions, and organizational principles need to shift toward processes being performed and the customers being served as organizing principles. The greatest challenges lie not in determining the boxes on a table of organization, but in sustaining the vision and commitment required to realize the benefits of these changes.

Academic Renewal at Michigan 7

James Duderstadt

This chapter originally appeared as Issue 1 of NACUBO's Executive Strategies series, a joint publication of NACUBO and the Stanford Forum for Higher Education Futures. It is based on Duderstadt's keynote address at the fall 1994 Stanford Forum symposium "Revitalizing our Institutions."

Over the last year I've run a simple experiment. I've asked various groups to assess the degree of change they believe universities will undergo during the 1990s, ranked on a scale from 0 to 10, with zero as the status quo and 10, radical change. I have found that faculty generally respond with estimates of three or four—there will be change but nothing earthshaking. Academic administrators—deans, provosts, and the like—tend to believe there will be more radical change, say on the order of seven or eight on the 10-point scale. But when I ask university presidents the same question, their responses bound off the scale: their average assessment is that the magnitude of change in our institutions will be about a 20! My own sense is that's about right.

Where We Are and How We Got Here

Before exploring change in higher education, it is helpful to understand what the modern research university has become. Part of the dilemma is that very few people, on campus or off, know. The public tends to think of the university in a very traditional way, with students sitting in large classrooms listening to senior faculty members lecture on Shakespeare.

The faculty thinks of Oxbridge—themselves as dons, and their students as serious scholars. The federal government sees just another research and development contractor or healthcare provider—a supplicant for the public purse. A brief analysis of the research university's mission shows the reality is far more complex. The classic triad of education, research, and service branches extensively, as shown in figure 7-1.

Figure 7-1: Triad Branching

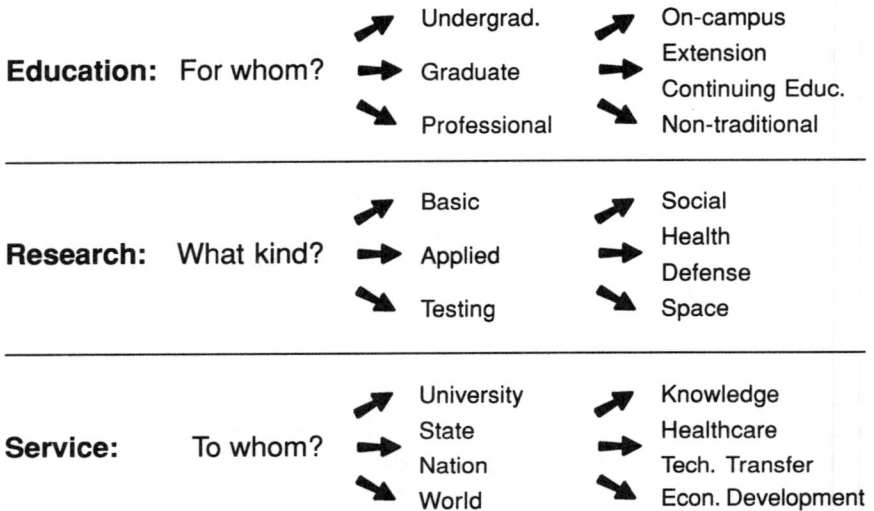

Education:	For whom?	⬀ Undergrad. ➡ Graduate ⬊ Professional	⬀ On-campus ➡ Extension Continuing Educ. ⬊ Non-traditional		
Research:	What kind?	⬀ Basic ➡ Applied ⬊ Testing	⬀ Social ➡ Health Defense ⬊ Space		
Service:	To whom?	⬀ University ➡ State Nation ⬊ World	⬀ Knowledge ➡ Healthcare Tech. Transfer ⬊ Econ. Development		

Let me suggest the image of the modern research university as a complex, international conglomerate of highly diverse businesses. My school, the University of Michigan (UM), for example, might be diagrammed as shown in figure 7-2. With an annual budget of over $2.5 billion, "The University of Michigan, Inc." would rank roughly 200th on the Fortune 500 list. Our several campuses educate about 50,000 students at an operating cost of about $800 million a year. We are a major federal R&D laboratory with over $400 million a year in grants and contracts. We run a massive healthcare company: our medical center treated over 800,000 patients last year and our managed-care operation comprises 70,000 "managed lives."

Last December we formed a nonprofit entity, the Michigan Health Corporation, that will allow us to make equity investments in joint ventures. Through it, we will build a statewide integrated healthcare system of roughly 1,500,000 subscribers—the population size we believe necessary to keep our university-owned tertiary hospitals afloat.

We also have our own captive insurance company since we are too big to buy insurance. And, we are actively involved in providing a wide array of knowledge services—from degree programs offered in Hong Kong, Seoul, and Paris to cyberspace-based activities such as managing part of the Internet. Finally, we are also involved in enter-

Figure 7-2: The University of Michigan, Inc.

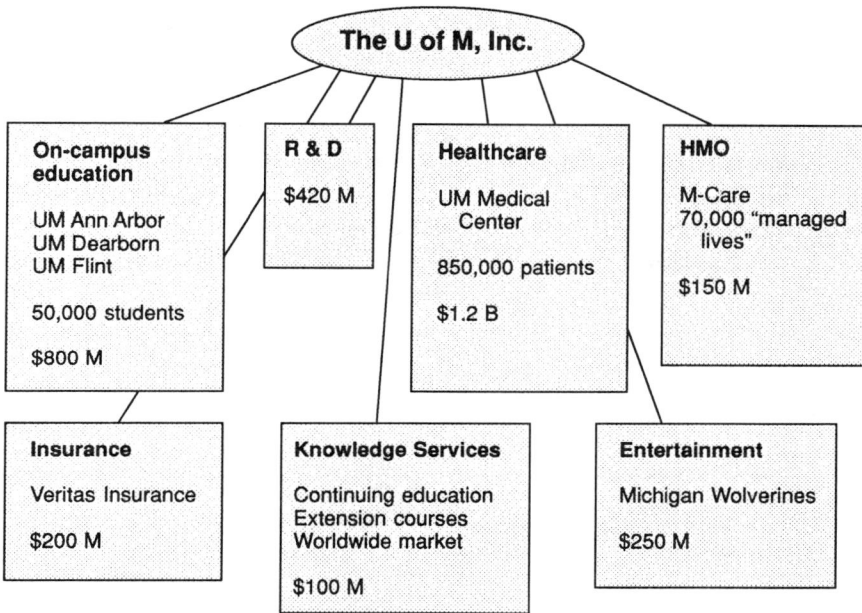

```
                        ┌─────────────────────────┐
                        │      The U of M, Inc.    │
                        └─────────────────────────┘
```

On-campus education	R & D	Healthcare	HMO
UM Ann Arbor	$420 M	UM Medical Center	M-Care 70,000 "managed lives"
UM Dearborn			
UM Flint		850,000 patients	$150 M
50,000 students		$1.2 B	
$800 M			

Insurance	Knowledge Services	Entertainment
Veritas Insurance	Continuing education Extension courses Worldwide market	Michigan Wolverines
$200 M		$250 M
	$100 M	

tainment—the Michigan Wolverines. The $250 million under "Michigan Wolverines" in figure 7-2 is not, thankfully, our athletic budget, but represents licensing and everthing else we do in this area. For example, recently we became the first university to sign a university-wide shoe contract with Nike, Inc., in an effort to pull in all of our various coaches' contracts.

This kind of "corporate" organization chart would describe many of the large research universities across the nation. We have all become conglomerates because of the interests and efforts of our faculty. We are prime examples of loosely coupled, adaptive systems that have grown in complexity as their various components have responded to environmental changes—each component pursuing its own particular goals. We are a "learning organization," to use the business term. Beyond that, we are also a holding company for thousands of faculty entrepreneurs.

Our character provides us with considerable resilience. Over the years we have responded to change and evolved to excel—driven by the creativity, effort, and energy of individual faculty and the units with which they identify, and by a transactional culture in which everything is negotiable—"let's make a deal" writ large. Figure 7-3 below describes this evolution in terms of The U of M, Inc.

But there are some problems with this reality. We may be in danger of diluting our core businesses of teaching and scholarship by engaging in so many diverse activities. And we have demonstrated a remarkable inability to eliminate outmoded and obsolete activities. Consequently, considerable underbrush clogs our enterprise even as we grow. Outdated policies, procedures, and practices increasingly stifle our best and most creative people.

As we consider change in higher education, it is important to keep in mind the extent to which the modern research university has grown and branched, and the challenges it faces as a result in shaping a successful future.

Figure 7-3: Evolution of The U of M, Inc.

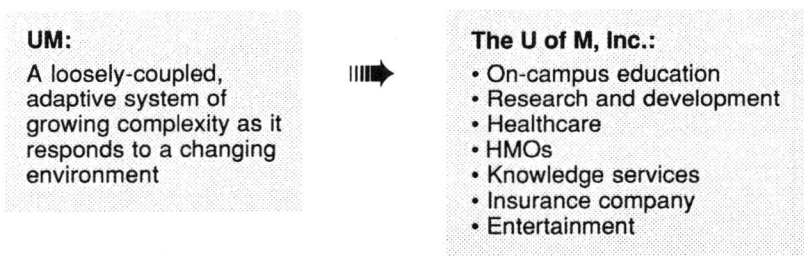

UM:
A loosely-coupled, adaptive system of growing complexity as it responds to a changing environment

The U of M, Inc.:
• On-campus education
• Research and development
• Healthcare
• HMOs
• Knowledge services
• Insurance company
• Entertainment

Natural evolution characterized by:
• a transactional culture
• decentralization with optimization at the level of individual units
• little attention to core mission or fundamental values

Concerns with The U of M, Inc.:
• dilution of "core businesses"
• so complex that few understand totality
• unable to eliminate outmoded and obsolete activities
• best people hindered byoutdated policies, procedures, practices

The Challenge of Change

Change is nothing new to higher education. As one of civilization's most enduring institutions, the university has been quite extraordinary in its capacity to change and adapt to serve society. Far from being immutable, the university has changed considerably over time and continues to do so today. A simple glance at the remarkable diversity of institutions comprising higher education in America demonstrates this evolution.

The profound nature of the challenges and changes facing higher education in the 1990s compares in significance to two other periods of great change in the nature of the American university: the late 19th century when comprehensive public universities first appeared, and the years following World War II when research universities evolved to serve the needs of postwar America.

A century ago, the industrial revolution was transforming our nation from an agrarian society into the industrial giant that would dominate the 20th century. The original colonial colleges, based on the elitist educational principles of Oxbridge, were joined by land-grant public universities committed to broad educational access and service to society. Higher education saw massive growth in merit-based enrollments at the undergraduate, graduate, and professional level as comprehensive universities subsequently evolved.

A similar period of rapid change occurred after World War II. The educational needs of returning veterans, the role of universities in national defense, and the booming postwar economy led to an explosion in both the size and number of major universities. So, too, the direct involvement of the federal government in the support of campus-based research led to the evolution of the research university as we know it today.

We now face challenges and opportunities similar to those of these earlier periods of transformation. Many observers focus on immediate challenges such as the rapidly growing costs of quality education and research during a period of limited resources, the erosion of public trust and confidence in higher education, or the deterioration in the relationship between research universities and the federal government. But our institutions will be affected more profoundly by powerful societal changes driving transformation: the increasing ethnic and cultural diversity of our people, the growing interdependence of nations, and the degree to which knowledge itself has become the key driving force in determining economic prosperity, national security, and social well-being.

One frequently thinks of the primary missions of the university in terms of teaching, research, and service. But these roles can also be regarded as simply the 20th century manifestations of the more fundamental roles of creating, preserving, integrating, transmitting, and applying knowledge. And while it is clear that these fundamental university roles have not changed over time, the way in which these missions have been realized has changed dramatically.

Consider, for example, the role of teaching (i.e., transmitting knowledge). While we generally think of a professor teaching to a classroom of students who read assigned texts, write papers, solve problems or perform experiments, and take examinations, this type of instruction is a relatively recent form of pedagogy. Throughout the last millennium, the more common form of learning was through apprenticeship. Both the neophyte scholar and craftsman learned by working as apprentices to a master. While one-on-one learning still occurs today in skilled professions such as medicine and in advanced education programs such as the Ph.D. dissertation, it is simply too labor-intensive for the mass educational needs of modern society.

The classroom itself may soon be replaced by more appropriate and efficient learning experiences. Indeed, such a paradigm shift may be forced upon the faculty by the students themselves. Today's students are members of the "digital" generation. They have spent their early lives surrounded by robust, visual, electronic media—"Sesame Street," MTV, home computers, video games, cyberspace networks, and virtual reality. They approach learning as a "plug-and-play" experience, unaccustomed and unwilling to learn sequentially—to read the manual—and rather inclined to plunge in and learn through participation and experimentation. While this type of learning is much different from the sequential, pyramid approach of the traditional university curriculum, it may be far more effective for this generation, particularly when provided through a media-rich environment.

Hence, faculty members of the 21st century university could well be asked to set aside their roles as teachers to become designers of learning experiences, processes, and environments. Tomorrow's faculty may have to discard the present style of solitary learning experiences in which students tend to learn primarily on their own through reading, writing, and problem solving. Instead they may be asked to develop collective learning experiences in which students work and learn together, with the faculty member becoming more of a consultant or a coach than a teacher.

The process of research and scholarship—creating new knowledge—is also evolving rapidly away from the solitary researcher to scholarly teams spread over several disciplines. Indeed, is the concept of the disciplinary specialist really necessary—or even relevant—in a future where the most interesting and significant problems will require this kind of "big think" rather than "small think"? Who needs such specialists when intelligent software agents will be available to roam far and wide through robust networks containing the knowledge of the world, instantly and effortlessly extracting whatever a person wishes to know?

So, too, there is increasing pressure to draw research topics more directly from worldly experience and needs than from the curiosity of scholars. Furthermore, the nature of knowledge creation is shifting somewhat away from the analysis of what has been to the creation of what has never been—drawing more on the experience of the artist than upon analytical skills of the scientist.

The preservation of knowledge is one of the most rapidly changing functions of the university. The computer, or more precisely the digital convergence of various media, has already supplanted the printing press in impacting knowledge. For centuries the intellectual focal point of the university has been the library—civilization's knowledge preserved as a collection of written works. Yet today such knowledge exists in many forms beyond print. Text, graphics, sound, algorithms, virtual reality simulations exist literally "in the ether" as digital representations over worldwide networks, accessible to anyone, not just a privileged few in academe.

Finally, it is also clear that societal needs will continue to dictate great changes in the applications of knowledge it accepts from universities. Over the past several decades, universities have been asked to take the lead in applying knowledge across a wide array of activities—from providing healthcare and protecting the environment to rebuilding our cities and entertaining the public at large (although it is sometimes hard to understand how intercollegiate athletics represents knowledge application!).

Here we face a particular dilemma. The pace of change has become so rapid and the nature of change so profound that it becomes increasingly difficult to even sense the changes (although we certainly feel the consequences), much less understand them sufficiently to respond and adapt. Institutions such as universities and government agencies, which have been the traditional structures for intellectual pursuits, may turn out to be as obsolete and irrelevant to the future as the American corporation of the 1950s. There is clearly a

need to explore new social structures capable of sensing and understanding change, and engaging in the strategic processes necessary
to adapt to or control it.

Some Different Paradigms

To illustrate the profound nature of this challenge, it is interesting to consider new paradigms that might characterize the "university of the 21st century." Several of the more provocative are described
below.

Ten Paradigms for the 21st Century University

1. **The Hybrid Public-Private University:** A state-related but inde-
   pendent university that has a strong public character but is sup-
   ported primarily through resources it generates itself (e.g., tuition,
   federal grants, private giving, auxiliary enterprises).
   Key questions:
   • How does one preserve the public character of a privately
     financed institution?
   • How does a state-related university adequately represent the
     interests of its majority stakeholders (parents, patients, fed-
     eral agencies, donors)?
   • Can one sustain an institution of the size and breadth of our
     public universities on self-generated ("private") revenues
     alone?

2. **The World University:** A university that adapts to the emerging
   global culture and services worldwide demand for learning, al-
   beit within the context of a particular geographical area (e.g.,
   North America).
   Key questions:
   • What would be the mission and character of a world university?
   • Who, how, where would it teach?
   • What programs would it stress? How would they be organized?
   • What strategic alliances could be formed with other institu-
     tions?
   • Would this paradigm be compatible with our state and na-
     tional missions?

3. The Diverse University (or "Transversity"): A university that draws its intellectual strength and character from the rich diversity of humankind, providing a model for society of a pluralistic learning community in which people respect and tolerate diversity even as they live, work, and learn together as a community of scholars.
Key questions:
- What society should we strive to represent? The state? The nation? The world? The present? The future?
- What kind of diversity do we seek? Racial? Ethnic? Gender? Socioeconomic? Geographical? Intellectual? Political?
- How do we draw strength from diversity?
- How do we attempt to unite a diverse community?

4. The Cyberspace University: A university that links students, faculty, graduates, and knowledge resources throughout the world (and possibly even beyond) via a robust digital information network.
Key questions:
- Will the cyberspace university be localized in space and time or will it be a "meta structure" involving many people throughout their lives, wherever they may be?
- Is the concept of the specialist (disciplines or professions) likely to remain relevant in such a knowledge-rich environment?
- Will lifestyles in the academy (and elsewhere) become increasingly nomadic, with people living and traveling where they wish, taking their work and social relationships with them?
- Will knowledge become less of a resource and more of a medium in such a university?

5. The Creative University: A university that has shifted its primary focus from analytical disciplines and professions to creative activities (e.g., synthesizing materials atom by atom, genetically engineering new life forms, generating artificial intelligence or virtual reality by computer) as a result of technological advances that make analysis less challenging and sophisticated creativity tools more available.
Key questions:
- Will the "creative" disciplines and professions (e.g., art, music, architecture, engineering) acquire more significance ?
- How does one nurture and teach the art and skill of creation?

6. **The Divisionless University:** A more integrated, less specialized university that will evolve out of a growing perception among younger faculty that current disciplinary (and professional) structures are irrelevant to teaching, scholarship, and service activities. The divisionless university will use webs of virtual structures to provide both horizontal and vertical integration among disciplines and professions.

   Key questions:
   - Should we reverse the trend toward more specialized undergraduate degrees in favor of a "bachelor's of liberal learning"?
   - Has the Ph.D. itself become obsolete to the extent that it produces highly specialized clones of the present graduate faculty?
   - Should the basic disciplines be mixed among the professions? Many of the most exciting problems have always been generated through interaction with the "real world."
   - How do we develop, evaluate, and reward faculty who are generalists rather than specialists?

7. **The University College:** A unit within the complex environment of a comprehensive research university that represents an intensified focus on undergraduate education. It will draw creatively on the intellectual resources of the entire university: its scholars, libraries, museums, liberal programs, and its remarkable diversity of people, ideas, and endeavors.

   Key questions:
   - Should we shift from solitary to collective learning experiences?
   - How do we respond to the fact that the current generation of students is quite different from the faculty, both in cultural composition and styles of learning (e.g., the "plug and play" generation)?
   - Should we require all faculty on our campuses—including those from professional schools—to become involved in undergraduate education?

8. **The Lifelong University:** A university that addresses the entire continuum of education, from cradle to grave. It may form strategic alliances with other components of the educational system and commits to lifetime interaction with its students, providing them with the continuing education necessary to meet their evolving goals and needs.

Key questions:
- How would this lifetime education be delivered?
- How would the university relate to other components of the educational continuum?
- How would this "seamless web" approach relate to our current focus on well-defined degree programs?

9. **The New University:** A "university" within a university that serves as a laboratory for prototyping and testing innovative academic applications. This academic unit of students, faculty, and programs will provide the intellectual and programmatic framework for continual experimentation that helps shape the vision and refine the features of the future university.

Key questions:
- Should the New U be a laboratory or proving ground for various possible visions of the university, or should it be a more permanent part of the university that we try to keep 20 or 30 years ahead of its time?
- Would the New U be a physical or virtual structure?
- Should the New U be built around research or service?
- How would we select students and faculty for the New U?

10. **The Knowledge Server:** A university that broadly and innovatively defines its role as knowledge server—creating, preserving, transmitting, and applying knowledge—by forging beyond traditional 20th century notions of teaching, research, and service to embrace new approaches and technologies (e.g., digital convergence, collective learning, strategic research).

Key questions:
- Is the paradigm of classroom teaching only a temporary device for learning? After all, the apprenticeship model has dominated for most of the last millennium.
- What are the implications of digital convergence, which will provide the knowledge of the world in many forms—text, graphics, sound, algorithms, virtual reality simulations—distributed over worldwide networks accessible by anyone?
- Will our institutions be asked by society to take on new roles that respond to new priorities (e.g., economic competitiveness and global change)?

Of course, our institutions are unlikely to assume the form of any one of these models. But, as the diagram of a possible 21st century university in figure 7-4 shows, each paradigm reflects aspects that almost certainly will be a part of our character in the century ahead.

These paradigms suggest the extraordinary nature of the transformations that will be required in our universities in the years ahead. Just as they have so many times in the past, our institutions must continue to change and evolve if we are to continue to serve—and, indeed, remain relevant to·a rapidly changing world.

Some Lessons Learned

So how does an institution as large, complex, and tradition-bound as the modern research university go about transforming itself? Historically we have accomplished change using a variety of mechanisms: 1) "buying" change with additional resources; 2) laboriously building the consensus necessary for grassroots support of change; 3) changing key people; 4) finesse; 5) by stealth of night; 6) "Just do it!," that is, top-down decisions followed by rapid execution (following the old adage that "it is better to seek forgiveness than to ask permission").

But we will need a more strategic approach to stay the course while moving our institutions toward the paradigms likely to characterize higher education in the years ahead. Indeed, many institutions have already embarked on major transformation agendas similar to those characterizing the private sector. Some even use familiar language: "transforming," "restructuring," or even "re-inventing" their institutions. But, of course, herein lies one of the great challenges to universities. Since our various missions and our diverse array of constituencies give us a complexity far beyond that encountered in business or government, the process of institutional transformation is necessarily more complex.

Based on the experiences of both public and private sector organizations, several features of the transformation process should be recognized at the outset:

1. The real challenge in transforming is not usually financial or organizational, but cultural. Universities will need to transform a rigid set of habits, thoughts, and arrangements currently incapable of responding to change either rapidly or radically enough.

Figure 7-4: A Vision of the 21st Century University

START WITH THE FUNDAMENTALS
- Attract, retain, and sustain outstanding people
- Achieve and enhance academic excellence
- Optimize quality, breadth, scale, excellence, and innovation
- Retain sufficient autonomy to control own destiny
- Balance resource portfolio to support excellence
- "Keep the joint jumpin'"

PARADIGMS BASED ON THE VISION

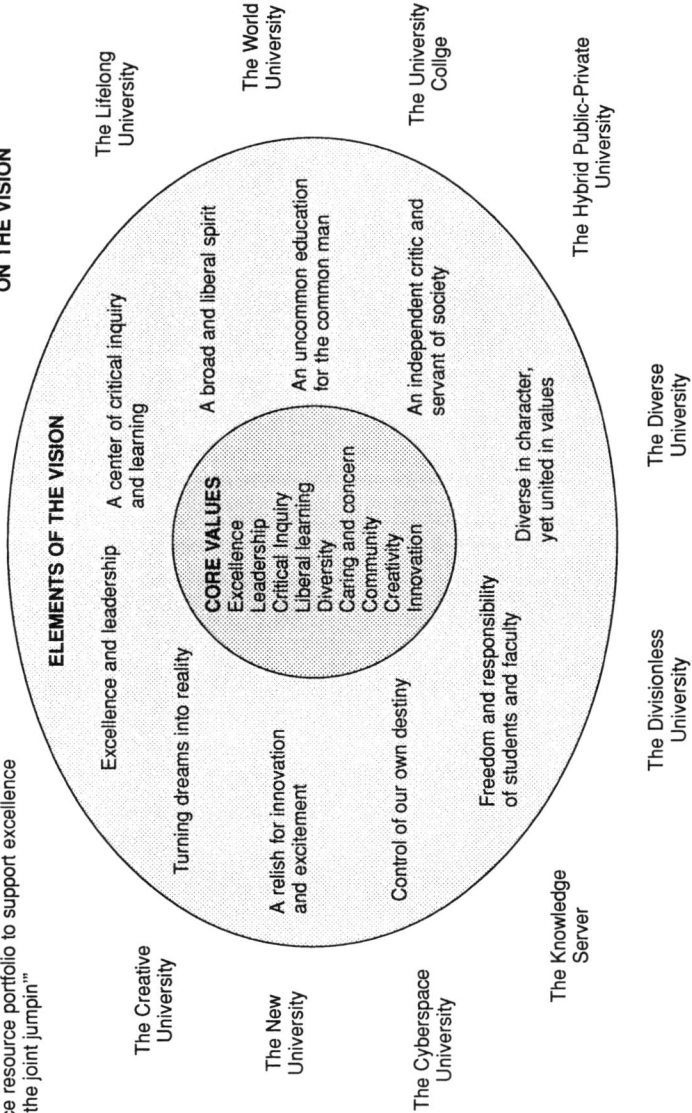

The Lifelong University

The World University

The University Collge

The Hybrid Public-Private University

The Diverse University

The Divisionless University

The Knowledge Server

The Cyberspace University

The New University

The Creative University

ELEMENTS OF THE VISION

Excellence and leadership

A center of critical inquiry and learning

A broad and liberal spirit

An uncommon education for the common man

An independent critic and servant of society

Diverse in character, yet united in values

Freedom and responsibility of students and faculty

Control of our own destiny

A relish for innovation and excitement

Turning dreams into reality

CORE VALUES
Excellence
Leadership
Critical Inquiry
Liberal learning
Diversity
Caring and concern
Community
Creativity
Innovation

2. True participation by key players in the design and implementation of the transformation process is essential. In the case of the university, special attention must be paid to involving the faculty—changing their culture will be the biggest challenge of all.
3. The use of an external group provides credibility to the transformation process. It is not only helpful but sometimes essential when putting controversial issues on the table (e.g., tenure reform).
4. It often takes a crisis for people to seriously consider transformation—and sometimes even this is not sufficient. Unfortunately, no universities—and few organizations in the private sector—have been able to achieve major change through the motivation of opportunity and excitement alone.
5. The organizational head must play a critical role as both leader and educator in designing, implementing, and selling the transformation process. University presidents in this role should particularly engage faculty in the process.

Experience demonstrates that organizational transformation is not only possible but even predictable to a degree. The revolutionary process starts with an analysis of the external environment and the recognition that radical change is the organization's best response to the challenges it faces. The early stages are sometimes turbulent—marked by conflict, denial, and resistance—but gradually, leaders and members of the organization begin to develop a shared vision of what their institution should become and turn their attention to the transformation process. In the final stages, grass-roots incentives and disincentives are put into place, creating internal market forces that drive institutional change. Methods are also developed that measure the success of the transformation process. Ideally, the process never ends.

The necessary transformations should go far beyond simply restructuring finances to face the brave new world of limited resources. Rather, they should encompass every aspect of our institutions including:

- The mission of the university
- Financial restructuring
- Organization and governance
- General characteristics of the university
- Intellectual transformation

- Relations with external constituencies
- Cultural change

Universities, like most large, complex, and hierarchical organizations, tend to become bureaucratic, conservative, and resistant to change. Over time we have become encrusted with policies, procedures, committees, and organizational layers that tend to discourage risk taking and creativity. We must take decisive action to streamline processes, procedures, and organizational structures to enable our institutions to better adapt to a rapidly changing world.

Conclusion

There is an increasing sense among American higher education's leaders and constituencies that the 1990s will represent a period of significant change on the part of our universities. If we are to respond successfully to the challenges, opportunities, and responsibilities before us, we will need to develop the capacity to transform ourselves using entirely new paradigms that better serve a rapidly changing society and a profoundly changing world.

We must seek to remove the constraints that prevent our institutions from responding promptly and flexibly. We must eliminate unnecessary processes and administrative structures, question existing premises and arrangements, and challenge, excite, and embolden the members of our university communities to embark on this great adventure. Our challenge is to work together to provide an environment in which such change is regarded not as a threat but as an exhilarating opportunity to engage in the primary activity of a university: learning—in all its many forms—to better serve our world.

The remarkable resilience of our institutions, their capacity to adapt to change, has existed in the past because in many ways they are intensely entrepreneurial, transactional cultures. We have provided our faculty the freedom, the encouragement, and the incentives to move toward their personal goals in highly flexible ways, and they have done so through good times and bad. Unfortunately, their efforts have frequently led today to organizations that are too comprehensive, complex, and detached from their core mission of learning.

The challenge is to tap this great source of creativity and energy associated with entrepreneurial activity in a way that preserves our fundamental mission and values. In a sense, we need to continue to encourage our tradition of natural evolution that has been so successful in responding to a changing world, but do so with greater strategic intent. Rather than continuing to evolve as an unconstrained transactional entrepreneurial culture, we need to guide this process to preserve our core missions, characteristics, and values. This strategic natural evolution of the university is described in the series of visions presented in figure 7-5.

We must also develop greater capacity to redirect our resources toward our highest priorities. While we are facing a period of more constrained resources, I believe that most of our institutions will continue to grow. After all, the knowledge business is a "growth industry." Yet, to use a gardening analogy, we need to develop the capacity to prune and shape this growth so that it is more strategic.

In summary, I share the sense among most of my colleagues as presidents of universities that the 1990s will see extraordinary changes in the nature of higher education and the nature of our institutions. A key element will be to provide ourselves with the flexibility and capacity to change in order to serve a changing society. But we must change in such a way that we preserve fundamental aspects of our characters and our values. This capacity for change—for renewal—is the key objective that we have to strive for in the years ahead. As the university has done many times in the past, it must transform itself again to meet the future.

Discussion

After his presentation at the Stanford Forum for Higher Education Futures Fall 1994 symposium, "Revitalizing Our Institutions," Duderstadt elaborated on his ideas in response to audience questioning. Excerpts from that conversation follow.

How can universities deal with "mission creep" when it's so hard to eliminate programs, and we have these low barriers to adding things? How are you going to move to one of those other paradigms? How are you going to release the best people and empower them to do something? Is that really possible?

The first question concerns focusing and refining our activities to bring them more in line with our core mission of learning. It seems clear that we need to learn the art of "mission shedding." That is, we

Figure 7-5: Strategic Natural Evolution of the University

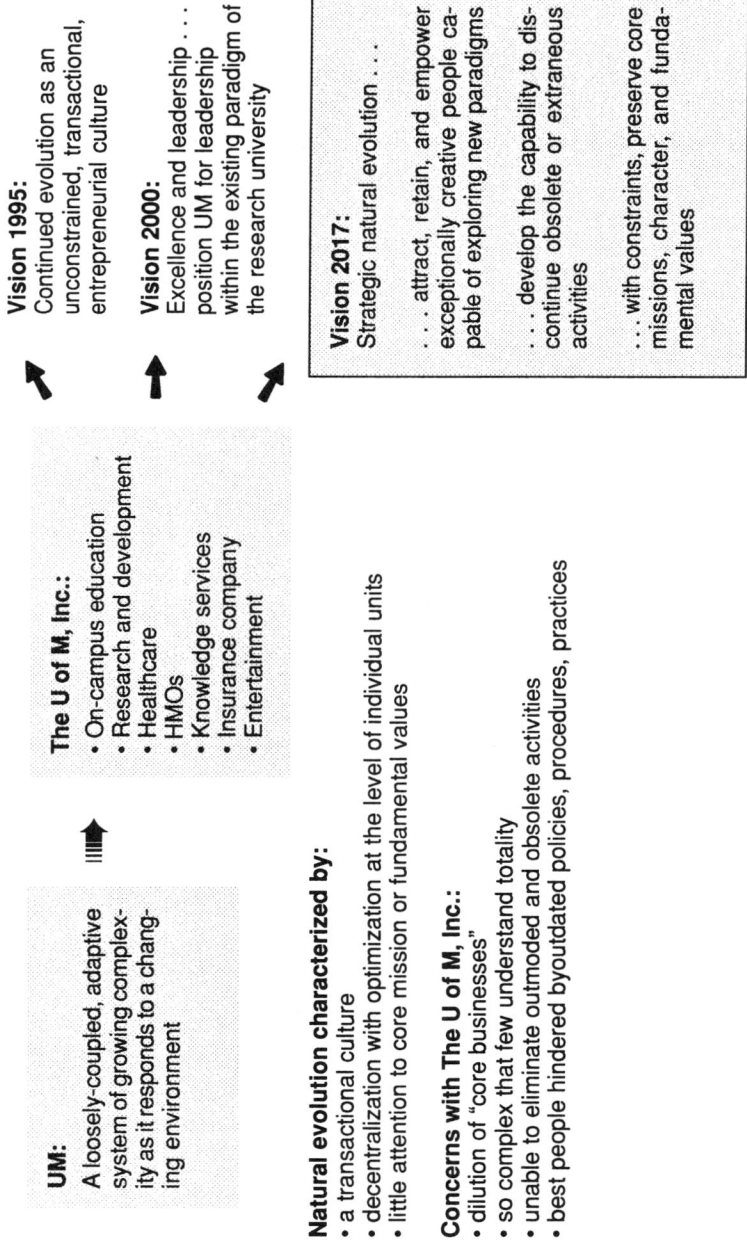

UM:

A loosely-coupled, adaptive system of growing complexity as it responds to a changing environment

The U of M, Inc.:

- On-campus education
- Research and development
- Healthcare
- HMOs
- Knowledge services
- Insurance company
- Entertainment

Natural evolution characterized by:

- a transactional culture
- decentralization with optimization at the level of individual units
- little attention to core mission or fundamental values

Concerns with The U of M, Inc.:

- dilution of "core businesses"
- so complex that few understand totality
- unable to eliminate outmoded and obsolete activities
- best people hindered by outdated policies, procedures, practices

Vision 1995:
Continued evolution as an unconstrained, transactional, entrepreneurial culture

Vision 2000:
Excellence and leadership . . . position UM for leadership within the existing paradigm of the research university

Vision 2017:
Strategic natural evolution . . .

. . . attract, retain, and empower exceptionally creative people capable of exploring new paradigms

. . . develop the capability to discontinue obsolete or extraneous activities

. . . with constraints, preserve core missions, character, and fundamental values

have to develop the capacity to shed some of the missions that we've taken on through the interest of our faculty in the past. Let me use an example. Like many institutions with large academic health centers, at Michigan we are building what will be a multi-billion-dollar healthcare system. Do we really need this size of operation to support our teaching and research mission? Of course not. But we do need a healthcare system this large to provide sufficient referrals to keep our massive tertiary and quadranary care hospitals afloat. Here we have an example of a mission that has probably outgrown our institution and needs to be spun off.

The answer to the second question of how to explore new paradigms depends on one's optimism about changing existing activities. Having been through a process in the early 1980s when we had to figure out how to adapt to a 30 percent loss in state appropriations over two years, I do not have a great deal of confidence in our capacity to change dramatically the way existing units function. Hence at Michigan we have been thinking more in terms of "from-scratch" or "green-field" experiments. One of the talking concepts has been that of a "new university," a skunk-works kind of laboratory in which we can try out possible paradigms of a university of the future. Of course, this is nothing new. In the 1950s and '60s the University of California did this in a big way by building entirely new campuses such as UC-Santa Cruz and UC-San Diego to explore new approaches to undergraduate and graduate education. But we are going a somewhat different route. First, we don't have the money that UC had at that time. Second, we don't have picturesque bluffs overlooking the Pacific. But, third, and most important, we don't believe that these green-field experiments developed apart from existing campuses have had the impact that they should have. Instead, we are designing the "new university" to be a virtual structure right in the center of our Ann Arbor campus. While it will have some quite unique facilities and organization, it will involve students and faculty from our mainstream programs. It will operate with different rules that encourage folks to try new things in a highly fault-tolerant environment. And, by being imbedded in the heart of our campus, we hope that successful experiments will propagate more rapidly through the rest of the university.

Maybe the new university approach will work, maybe it won't. But there is an important reason for such efforts. In the recent White House science policy paper "Science in the National Interest," a goal was suggested for a national investment in research and development comparable to 3 percent of the gross domestic product. In a similar fashion, most companies set their R&D budget at several percent of sales. Yet most universities spend far less than 1 percent of their general & education budget on researching better ways to improve the fundamental missions of teaching, research, and service. In reality, the concept of the new university suggests that we should increase this internal effort to several percent of G&E by investing in discovery and prototyping efforts that look to the future. We need to provide our most creative people not only with the support to explore new paradigms of the university, but fault-tolerant environments in which risk taking and adventure are encouraged.

Hearing about the merging of the libraries of the Big Ten is absolutely mind boggling. Any one of your libraries is mind boggling as it is. Is the future then in creating larger and larger and more and more complex entities to deal with a particular thing, or are we going to think maybe scale and size might go the other way, to be more efficient?

Technology may make scale less and less relevant. Even the efforts of the Big Ten to combine their libraries to achieve a 58-million-volume library will probably be obsolete quite soon. By the time we're finished, the Library of Congress will be on-line, available to every household in America. As size and scale become less relevant, alliances will become more important, and perhaps less traditional. The easiest alliances to think about are institutions of a like character coming together: Big Ten universities or the AAU universities and so forth. But what about an alliance between a university and a very different enterprise, such as Microsoft, Time Warner, Disney, Lucas Films? We actually have those under development right now. In a sense, these software and entertainment companies are educational institutions as well. Indeed, Microsoft may be the university of the future, marketing directly to the home. Such alliances will form and shape the nature of all the institutions that participate in them. For example, the World Wide Web is a gigantic alliance of thousands and thousands of institutions and millions and millions of people. We don't really understand this phenomenon yet, but it's growing like topsy—15 percent a month.

You've said that you thought it was wise perhaps to use outsiders to get the controversial issues on the table without jeopardizing the cred-

ibility of some of the people. Could you elaborate on that, maybe give us some examples?

Sure. David Ward, chancellor of the University of Wisconsin, was finally able to get his faculty senate to take post-tenure review seriously when he pointed out that the Wisconsin legislature was about ready to pass legislation that would force the issue. This represents both pressure and credibility on a sensitive issue. And apparently the Wisconsin faculty senate responded quite well to that challenge.

It can be done through visiting groups—trustees in some cases, although in public institutions you probably want people with broader experience than generally found on governing boards. It can also be provided through experts—management consultants such as McKinsey or Andersen Consulting—who can help in a serious redesign of how one manages a multi-billion-dollar university. Beyond the fact that they may give us some new ideas, they will also give us credibility from the outside that we can't generate inside. So it's all of the above: credibility, pressure, and wisdom. Multiple inputs.

Where is governance in this whole process? What about trustees, legislators, and other publics who don't even understand us now? What about faculty governance?

The issue of governance is a very serious one, particularly for public institutions. Since most public boards are selected through partisan political mechanisms—at Michigan, through statewide general elections—they generally view themselves more as guardians for the public's interest rather than as trustees for the university. Further, the political selection process rarely yields boards with the broad experience and influence characterizing private universities. Finally, the onerous sunshine laws constraining the operation of public boards make very difficult the confidential discussions necessary to consider the complex issues associated with institutional change.

At Michigan we are thinking of restructuring our corporate organization more along the lines of a holding company model. In such a model, the formal governing board and leadership of the institution becomes a fairly small organization dealing with broad policy issues. The components of the institution will be diverse: nonprofit or for-profit, publicly regulated or unregulated, for example. These could have interlocking boards, sometimes internal, sometimes with external directors. Such a decentralized approach to our various missions might give our various components far more autonomy and freedom. In certain of our activities—commercial licensing, health-care, and so forth—we're simply going to have to do that. These activities operate in intensely competitive worlds. In terms of academic institutions, we have community-based campuses, for example in Flint and Dearborn, that really need to have community-based governing. They should not be governed by a board that is primarily concerned with the flagship campus in Ann Arbor.

What about faculty governance? That is a difficult question. How does the faculty "govern" a two-billion-dollar-per-year healthcare system, for example? When one has to worry about the bottom line, faculty governance becomes problematic. Governance must be accompanied by accountability. And I suppose if the faculty is willing to accept fiduciary responsibility and accountability they can be involved, but until they are, they may find themselves increasingly out of the decision making for many of these activities.

How can universities engage their faculty in academic restructuring?

We need to expose our faculty to a sense of reality. Consider the clinical faculty in our medical school, who have already faced dramatic change. As the compensation levels of our specialists, thoracic surgeons, radiologists, and so forth began to plummet, the faculty sensed something had changed. They saw the writing on the wall and came to us for help. Other parts of the institution, particularly in the liberal arts, are much more buffered from change and are having some difficulty in understanding what's happening—even sensing that things are changing. In those cases we really have to bring thought leaders to our campuses to engage faculty in a consideration of change. We're going through such a process right now with Bob Zemsky of the Pew Higher Education Roundtable that many of you have also experienced. In our case, rather than put together faculty leaders, we brought together 20 junior faculty that had just achieved tenure to see how they grapple with restructuring issues. It's been a very educational experience. We've learned a lot and they've learned a lot. But we have also learned that such discussions have to occur in a variety of different ways—different strokes for different folks. We do find that our professional schools understand much better the kind of changes that are underway and the extraordinary nature of the transformations that they're going to have to undergo because they're at the boundary between the institution and society. For example, some of our professional schools are beginning to reconsider whether tenure has become an archaic concept. In other schools, the fine arts for example, tenure may disappear because of the increasing use of artists-in-residence who remain on campus for only a brief period. The important thing is to realize the extraordinary diversity of our campuses and our activities and recognize that you need a diversity in faculty roles and in the faculty contract.

Sometimes you use the word "constraints," and one context was in student contact with cumbersome administrative procedures. We need to get rid of constraints. Could you talk a bit about that? On the other hand, you use the word "management" and that we've got to move strategically. Could you also address that?

Part of the challenge is to clear the underbrush cluttering our institutions. Like all institutions, we have a thicket of policies and procedures and practices, along with the anarchy of committee and consensus decision making—which is an oxymoron in itself. Committees don't make decisions. Our best people now feel quite constrained by the university as it is currently defined, constrained by their colleagues, constrained by the "administration," but beyond that, even as we remove those constraints, there have to be some mechanisms in place to guide the institution in a strategic way. That will be done in different ways by different institutions.

At our institution, the provost, Gil Whitaker, is leading the difficult process of moving us to responsibility center management. We've had a highly decentralized institution for many years which has been operated according to centralized fund accounting. There have been few direct incentives to guide behavior or control costs at the unit level. We hope that responsibility center management will accomplish three things: (1) provide strong incentives for individual units to generate resources; (2) provide strong incentives for units to use those resources wisely; and (3) give the central administration more capacity to guide the institution by providing significant resources under its control, much of which will be returned as conscious subsidies—"strengthening the tiller" as it were. Michigan may be somewhat unique in that because we already have a highly decentralized management, to move strategically we may to have to centralize a bit more control over resources. That does not go down easily with many of our deans, who resist such budgeting changes.

In any one of these initiatives you described, you're going to have to make major bets, major investments—millions, maybe hundreds of millions of dollars—and then wait awhile to see how they work. What are the chances that, over a decade or two, you're going to make a mistake that will threaten the organization?

Well I hope that the chance of making a mistake is 100 percent because if you don't fall on your face from time to time, you're not really shooting high enough.

When you talk about hundreds of millions of dollars, you know, it catches our attention.

That's right. Well, actually we're about to make a $50 million bet on the "new university" concept, and another $100 million bet on a new joint healthcare venture. It depends a lot on the scale of the institution, but I do think you have to create an environment in which you're willing to take significant risks. Indeed, you have to take risks both with respect to resources and with respect to the political environment of the campus. Perhaps that is why the tenure of presidents of major research universities has become so short. A case in point: during the past two years, seven of the 11 Big Ten presidents have stepped down. To survive over five years at the helm of a major public institution is a real accomplishment. Maybe we need a lot of different kinds of perspectives and viewpoints. In our case, we're making some very significant bets, creating laboratories in which exciting things are happening.

We are spending $50 million on a new facility that is portrayed as a library and learning center—except it has no books, no classrooms, and no faculty. It will be a merger of art, music, architecture, engineering, and computer science, designed to focus on the activity of creation. Some really exciting faculty and students want to do this. It's a neat thing to try, but of a scale that is probably larger than a lot of institutions could handle. Recall I used the goal of 3 percent of the G&E budget as the target for university "corporate R&D" efforts. For us, that's about $30 million a year, and that probably is the right kind of scale. We should be prepared to make those kinds of bets.

Can we assume the 10 percent contribution Michigan receives from the state leads a lot of people at the state level to think that means 100 percent accountability and control?

They're inversely related actually.

How do you talk about these matters with folks in the state government? How do you talk about the conflict between institutional autonomy and what they're doing?

Very carefully. This is one of those issues that you can probably talk to Republicans about better than you can to Democrats. Republicans tend to like this idea of privatizing. Democrats tend more toward public control. It is a very difficult matter because the people on the street in Detroit or Saginaw believe they own the University of Michigan. Yet, in terms of actual support, they pay for only about one-tenth of our operations, which makes them our smallest minority shareholders. Yet, technically, they still own us. We believe that state support will be down to about 5 percent of our operating budget by the end of this decade, yet state regulations and political bonds will become even more intrusive. Already, for example, the sunshine laws—open meetings acts and freedom of information laws—are crippling the operation of public institutions. Many people, including members of the media, are well aware of the dangers these pose to universities, yet the press continues to hammer away for even more intrusive laws.

I do believe that we're on a trajectory right now where the most distinguished and comprehensive of public universities—perhaps as many as 20 to 30—will be forced by the erosion of public support to operate as public-private hybrid institutions if they are to maintain their quality. Perhaps Cornell is the model for our future. I suppose the University of Pennsylvania is the extreme as another model. They've gone 50 to 100 years past Cornell, and they're now almost entirely private. I hope it doesn't go to that extreme, but I think you will see that kind of evolution, and how you handle the politics is going to be very, very difficult.

The tenure of a university president is shorter than it used to be, but it seems that the implications of what you've been saying is that you need sustained leadership to accomplish change. Do you want to talk a little about this?

I think it is quite troubling about the tenure of the university presidents. I'm sure there are far better ways to get lots of new ideas into an institution without turning over its leadership every three or four years, but that seems to be what's happened during the 1980s and 1990s. Part of the turnover is due to external pressures on higher education, but much of it is from pure politics—politics from within and politics from without. The role of the university president is a very hazardous one these days. MIT's Paul Gray used to say that the definition of a modern university president was someone who lived in a large house and begged for a living. But I think that a better analogy to the role of the university president these days is the local sheriff in a frontier town who has to get up every morning and strap his guns on and go out in the main street and see what gunslingers have roamed into town to shoot the place up. One of these days, you're going to meet someone faster at the draw than you are. So be it.

Let's go back to the issue of crisis. You mentioned that having a crisis was important for initiating change, yet you've also talked about things that are changing and you've made a lot of progress. Does that mean the institution is no longer in a crisis, was never in a crisis, is beyond a crisis?

It depends enormously on the institution. The University of Michigan has not been in crisis. We had a scare in the early '80s, but we certainly don't have a crisis now. And yet, I worry whether you can achieve the degree of change that you need without some degree of anxiety or even fear. I worry about that. I would like to think that opportunity and hope and excitement can motivate people to change. But sometimes it takes a wolf at the door to get their attention. What happens if you don't have a convenient wolf nearby? Do you have to create one? I don't know. We're trying lots of things, but whether we can achieve the degree of change we need without the wolf at the door—we continue to have doubts.

You mentioned pruning a bush, "slowly but surely." Can you give me an example, from the academic side of the house, of a bush you've pruned—and also maybe a new bush you planted that didn't turn out as successful as you thought?

We've made plenty of mistakes—although we usually don't let the papers get word of this up to East Lansing. I think we made some big mistakes during the early 1980s when we tried to put into place a very public mechanism capable of discontinuing academic programs. Actually at that time we tried to discontinue three schools and a number of subprograms, but in the end, didn't really discontinue anything. We did cut them down at the cost of great trauma. But we learned that a public lynching in the town square just did not work. We're now trying to learn how to prune in different ways. What we're learning is that, at least in a highly public institution governed by strong sunshine laws, we really have to accomplish the pruning by finesse, by reorganizing units and hoping that in the process, units just disappear. This sounds somewhat Machiavellian, but that may be the only way to do it. For example, we've just gone through a process of eliminating for the second time our Population Planning Department. It was eliminated during the late 1970s, but it grew back in the 1980s. When we tried to eliminate it again using a public process, we found that we just couldn't do it. So what we finally ended up doing is restructuring the parent body, our School of Public Health, by reorganizing it from eight departments into four departments. In the process, we magically lost population planning, but in an acceptable fashion. So I suppose sleight of hand may be a good approach. But I don't look at Michigan as a good model for such efforts. I understand that UCLA is going through a similar pruning process again using reorganization as the mechanism to restructure and eliminate.

You talked about the relationship between what the leaders of the institution are doing and what it takes to be a change agent. I've agreed with everything you've said, which takes me to the relationship between the institution and its faculty. I'm concerned about the growth in part-time faculty. Certain activities need to grow, but we want to be flexible and we don't want to build in all that tenure. For example, you or somebody earlier mentioned performing arts faculty and maybe other professions where tenure isn't important. This really isn't a tenure issue I'm raising. I'm raising the issue of full-time versus part-time employment. Industry is going more and more to contract employees, and I worry about such key people as the clinical faculty becoming part-time employees. I wonder if you would comment on this in relation to the other issues that are driving the university?

I think the key feature that all institutions in our society are driving for is flexibility, increased flexibility to deal with a rapidly changing world. Those institutions that are not capable of achieving flexibility are going to decline and perhaps disappear. They're going to be swept aside.

In the corporate sector, they've achieved more flexibility by decreasing the number of permanent long-term employees and making far more use of part-time flexible employees to deal with certain missions. This is also clearly happening in higher education. Most of our institutions are making far more use of flexible staff—lecturers, research scientists, clinical faculty—rather than tenure-track faculty. This creates a very serious personnel problem, of course. But I suspect that universities will follow courses similar to those pursued in other sectors. We will inevitably be driven toward a smaller and smaller core of permanent individuals, whether it be faculty or staff, using more and more in the way of people that come in for limited periods of time to address various missions that tend to change. That is the nature of the times in which we live, and I think that if we don't move toward that we're going to become so ponderous and resistant to change that our viability is going to be threatened.

It would be great if changes swirling about higher education were on a slower time scale than in the rest of our society, but this simply isn't the case. It always amazes me how rapidly companies are able to respond when the alternative is Chapter 11. Both complex decisions and complex execution can occur on the time scale of weeks or even days. The glacial time scales characterizing the university decision process are simply no longer acceptable. We simply cannot survive in this time of change unless we ourselves are capable of far more dramatic and rapid change.

About the Contributors

Neal F. Binstock is the assistant vice president for business services at Carnegie Mellon University. Binstock has been with Carnegie Mellon for 22 years in various positions, including assistant dean for the Graduate School of Industrial Administration and director of administration for Facilities. He also received his education from Carnegie Mellon.

L. Edwin Coate, Ph.D., is the vice president for business services at MiraCosta College. Before joining MiraCosta, Coate held similar positions at the University of California, Santa Cruz, and Oregon State University. He has done extensive pioneering work with total qualtity management and business process redesign, and is the author of several publications on the subject, including NACUBO's recently released *change@ucsc.edu* and two papers in the NACUBO Effective Management series. He received a bachelor's degree in public administration from San Diego State University and his doctorate in human behavior from the United States International University

James Duderstadt, Ph.D., is the president of the University of Michigan. Duderstadt has been with the University of Michigan since 1968, serving 12 years as a faculty member before becoming the dean of engineering in 1981 and then provost and vice president for academic affairs in 1986. He was elected president in 1988. Duderstadt received his bacculaureate degree in electric engineering from Yale University and his doctorate in engineering from the California Institute of Technology.

John A. Fry, AB, MBA, is formerly a partner at Coopers & Lybrand L.L.P., where he served as National Director of Consulting Services for Higher Education. He has over ten years of experience working with colleges and universities in the areas of organizational restructuring, strategic planning, and productivity improvement. Fry has served as a management instructor at New York University's Stern School of business and at the Graduate Program at Hunter College of the City of New York. Fry recently left Coopers & Lybrand to become the executive vice president of the University of Pennsylvania.

Philip J. Goldstein is a managing associate in Coopers & Lybrand's national Higher Education Consulting Practice. He has more than five years experience in the higher education industry, specializing in business process re-engineering, organizational design, and technology implementation. Goldstein is a frequent speaker at NACUBO annual meetings, as well as those of APPA and NACAS. He holds a B.A. in economics from Brandeis University and an MBA from New York University's Stern School of Business.

Myron S. Henry, Ph.D., has been the provost at Kent State University since 1992. Prior to joining Kent State, he served as chief academic officer at Old Dominion University. He has delivered numerous presentations on academic strategic planning, resource allocation processes, and the politics of budget reductions in fiscally constrained times. He holds a B.S. from Ball State University, and M.S. and Ph.D. degrees in mathematics from Colorado State University.

Patrick J. Keating, Ph.D., is vice president for business affairs and university planning at Carnegie Mellon University. Keating began his career at Carnegie Mellon as director of university planning in 1983, became vice president of university planning in 1988, and assumed his current position in 1990. He received his B.A. in economics and a Ph.D. in higher education administration from Michigan State University. Keating also holds an M.P.P. in public policies studies from the University of Michigan.

Jillinda J. Kidwell is a director in Coopers & Lybrand L.L.P.'s Higher Education Consulting Practice, where she is responsible for the firm's West Coast and Midwest college and university consulting engagements. Kidwell pioneered the application of reengineering methods to campus settings, and is co-author of two NACUBO publications: *Measurement Systems in Higher Education* (NACUBO Effective Management Series) and *Business Process Redesign in Higher Education.*

Alfonso de Lucio is a senior associate at Coopers & Lybrand L.L.P.'s Higher Education Consulting Practice. Over the past three years, he has worked with colleges and universities in the area of business process re-engineering. Prior to joining Coopers & Lybrand, de Lucio was a senior manager for the NACUBO Center for Institutional Accounting, Finance, and Management.

Mary Jo Maydew, MBA, is treasurer and chief financial officer of Mount Holyoke College. Maydew came to Mount Holyoke in 1987 from Cornell University, where she held the positions of assistant treasurer and assistant to the university controller. She is currently second vice president of the Eastern Association of College and University Business Officers, and has served on that board since 1988. Maydew received a bachelor of science degree from the University of Denver and an MBA from Cornell University's Johnson Graduate School of Management.

David J. O'Brien is the director of the Office of Planning Services at the Stanford University School of Medicine. O'Brien has been at the Stanford University Medical Center since 1981, and has led a study of the school's administrative costs and alternative models for organization since early 1994. O'Brien received his master's degree in health administration from the University of Washington.

Paula M. Rooney, Ph.D., is president of Dean College. Prior to assuming her current position, Rooney was vice president of student affairs at Babson College.

P. Gerard Shaw, Ph.D., is a senior associate with Coopers & Lybrand's Higher Education Consulting Practice.

NACUBO Board of Directors

John A. Palmucci, Chair, Loyola College in Maryland

Jerry B. Farley, Vice Chair, University of Oklahoma

Janet Hamilton, Secretary, University of California, Davis

Karla Chappelle Howard, Treasurer

Mernoy E. Harrison, Immediate Past Chair, California State University, Sacramento

Daniel Boggan Jr., National Collegiate Athletic Association

R.W. "Pete" Denton, University of South Carolina

William M. Dixon, Wytheville Community College

James M. Dodson, McPherson College

Dennis F. Dougherty, University of Southern California

Nancy B. Eddy, Holyoke Community College

Thomas G. Estes, Mercer University

Emerson H. Fly, University of Tennessee

J. Peyton Fuller, Duke University

George F. Keane, The Common Fund

Katharine J. Kral, University of Illinois, Urbana/Champaign

Gina Kranitz, Paradise Valley Community College

William E. Lavery, Virginia Polytechnic Institute and State University

Edward R. MacKay, University System of New Hampshire

Jerry N. Wallace, University of Idaho

Wayne A. Warnecke, Lakeland College

James E. Morley Jr., NACUBO President